Pittsburgh Pirates 2020

A Baseball Companion

Edited by R.J. Anderson, Craig Goldstein and Bret Sayre

Baseball Prospectus

Craig Brown, Steven Goldman and David Pease, Consultant Editors
Robert Au, Harry Pavlidis and Amy Pircher, Statistics Editors

Copyright © 2020 by DIY Baseball, LLC.
All rights reserved

This book or any part thereof may not be reproduced or transmitted in any form or by any means, electronic or mechanical, including photocopying, recording, or by any information storage and retrieval system, without permission in writing from the publisher.

Limit of Liability/Disclaimer of Warranty: While the publisher and the author have used their best efforts in preparing this book, they make no representations or warranties with respect to the accuracy or completeness of the contents of this book and specifically disclaim any implied warranties of merchantability or fitness for a particular purpose. No warranty may be created or extended by sales representatives or written sales materials. The advice and strategies contained herein may not be suitable for your situation. You should consult with a professional where appropriate. Neither the publisher nor the author shall be liable for any loss of profit or any other commercial damages, including but not limited to special, incidental, consequential, or other damages.

Library of Congress Cataloging-in-Publication Data:
paperback
ISBN-13: 978-1-950716-14-2

Project Credits
Cover Design: Michael Byzewski at Aesthetic Apparatus
Interior Design and Production: Jeff Pease, Dave Pease
Layout: Jeff Pease, Dave Pease

Baseball icon courtesy of Uberux, from https://www.shareicon.net/author/uberux

Ballpark diagram courtesy of Lou Spirito/THIRTY81 Project, https://thirty81project.com/

Manufactured in the United States of America
10 9 8 7 6 5 4 3 2 1

Table of Contents

Statistical Introduction v

Part 1: Team Analysis

Pittsburgh Pirates: Where Are You Going, Where Have You Been? 3
    Brian Duricy, Ben Spanier and Matthew Trueblood

Performance Graphs 7

2019 Team Performance 8

2020 Team Projections 9

Team Personnel 10

PNC Park Stats 11

Pirates Team Analysis 13

Part 2: Player Analysis

Pirates Player Analysis 18

Pirates Prospects 113

Part 3: Featured Articles

The Baseball Is Juiced (Again) 127
    Robert Arthur

The Moral Hazard of Playing It Safe 131
    Craig Goldstein

Index of Names 137

Statistical Introduction

Sports are, fundamentally, a blend of athletic endeavor and storytelling. Baseball, like any other sport, tells its stories in so many ways: in the arc of a game from the stands or a season from the box scores, in photos, or even in numbers. At Baseball Prospectus, we understand that statistics don't replace observation or any of baseball's stories, but complement everything else that makes the game so much fun.

What stats help us with is with patterns and precision, variance and value. This book can help you learn things you may not see from watching a game or hundred, whether it's the path of a career over time or the breadth of the entire MLB. We'd also never ask you to choose between our numbers and the experience of viewing a game from the cheap seats or the comfort of your home; our publication combines running the numbers with observations and wisdom from some of the brightest minds we can find. But if you *do* want to learn more about the numbers beyond what's on the backs of player jerseys, let us help explain.

Offense

We've revised our methodology for determining batting value. Long-time readers of the book will notice that we've retired True Average in favor of a new metric: Deserved Runs Created Plus (DRC+). Developed by Jonathan Judge and our stats team, this statistic measures everything a player does at the plate–reaching base, hitting for power, making outs, and moving runners over–and puts it on a scale where 100 equals league-average performance. A DRC+ of 150 is terrific, a DRC+ of 100 is average and a DRC+ of 75 means you better be an excellent defender.

DRC+ also does a better job than any of our previous metrics in taking contextual factors into account. The model adjusts for how the park affects performance, but also for things like the talent of the opposing pitcher, value of different types of batted-ball events, league, temperature and other factors. It's able to describe a player's expected offensive contribution than any other statistic we've found over the years, and also does a better job of predicting future performance as well.

There's a lot more to DRC+'s story, and you can read all about it in greater depth near the end of this book.

The other aspect of run-scoring is baserunning, which we quantify using Baserunning Runs. BRR not only records the value of stolen bases (or getting caught in the act), but also accounts for all the stuff that doesn't show up on the back of a baseball card: a runner's ability to go first to third on a single, or advance on a fly ball.

Defense

Where offensive value is *relatively* easy to identify and understand, defensive value is…not. Over the past dozen years, the sabermetric community has focused mostly on stats based on zone data: a real-live human person records the type of batted ball and estimated landing location, and models are created that give expected outs. From there, you can compare fielders' actual outs to those expected ones. Simple, right?

Unfortunately, zone data has two major issues. First, zone data is recorded by commercial data providers who keep the raw data private unless you pay for it. (All the statistics we build in this book and on our website use public data as inputs.) That hurts our ability to test assumptions or duplicate results. Second, over the years it has become apparent that there's quite a bit of "noise" in zone-based fielding analysis. Sometimes the conclusions drawn from zone data don't hold up to scrutiny, and sometimes the different data provided by different providers don't look anything alike, giving wildly different results. Sometimes the hard-working professional stringers or scorers might unknowingly inflict unconscious bias into the mix: for example good fielders will often be credited with more expected outs despite the data, and ballparks with high press boxes tend to score more line drives than ones with a lower press box.

Enter our Fielding Runs Above Average (FRAA). For most positions, FRAA is built from play-by-play data, which allows us to avoid the subjectivity found in many other fielding metrics. The idea is this: count how many fielding plays are made by a given player and compare that to expected plays for an average fielder at their position (based on pitcher ground ball tendencies and batter handedness). Then we adjust for park and base-out situations.

When it comes to catchers, our methodology is a little different thanks to the laundry list of responsibilities they're tasked with beyond just, well, catching and throwing the ball. By now you've probably heard about "framing" or the art of making umpires more likely to call balls outside the strike zone for strikes. To put this into one tidy number, we incorporate pitch tracking data (for the years it exists) and adjust for important factors like pitcher, umpire, batter and home-field advantage using a mixed-model approach. This grants us a number for how many strikes the catcher is personally adding to (or subtracting from) his pitchers' performance…which we then convert to runs added or lost using linear weights.

Framing is one of the biggest parts of determining catcher value, but we also take into account blocking balls from going past, whether a scorer deems it a passed ball or a wild pitch. We use a similar approach—one that really benefits from the pitch tracking data that tells us what ends up in the dirt and what doesn't. We also include a catcher's ability to prevent stolen bases and how well they field balls in play, and *finally* we come up with our FRAA for catchers.

Pitching

Both pitching and fielding make up the half of baseball that isn't run scoring: run prevention. Separating pitching from fielding is a tough task, and most recent pitching analysis has branched off from Voros McCracken's famous (and controversial) statement, "There is little if any difference among major-league pitchers in their ability to prevent hits on balls hit in the field of play." The research of the analytic community has validated this to some extent, and there are a host of "defense-independent" pitching measures that have been developed to try and extract the effect of the defense behind a hurler from the pitcher's work.

Our solution to this quandary is Deserved Run Average (DRA), our core pitching metric. DRA looks like earned run average (ERA), the tried-and-true pitching stat you've seen on every baseball broadcast or box score from the past century, but it's very different. To start, DRA takes an event-by-event look at what the pitchers does, and adjusts the value of that event based on different environmental factors like park, batter, catcher, umpire, base-out situation, run differential, inning, defense, home field advantage, pitcher role and temperature. That mixed model gives us a pitcher's expected contribution, similar to what we do for our DRC+ model for hitters and FRAA model for catchers. (Oh, and we also consider the pitcher's effect on basestealing and on balls getting past the catcher.)

It's important to note that DRA is set to the scale of runs allowed per nine innings (RA9) instead of ERA, which makes DRA's scale slightly higher than ERA's. The reason for this is because ERA tends to overrate three types of pitchers:

1. Pitchers who play in parks where scorers hand out more errors. Official scorers differ significantly in the frequency at which they assign errors to fielders.
2. Ground-ball pitchers, because a substantial proportion of errors occur on groundballs.
3. Pitchers who aren't very good. Better pitchers often allow fewer unearned runs than bad pitchers, because good pitchers tend to find ways to get out of jams.

Since the last time you picked up an edition of this book, we've also made a few minor changes to DRA to make it better. Recent research into "tunneling"—the act of throwing consecutive pitches that appear similar from a batter's point of view until after the swing decision point–data has given us a new contextual factor to account for in DRA: plate distance. This refers to the distance between successive pitches as they approach the plate, and while it has a smaller effect than factors like velocity or whiff rate, it still can help explain pitcher strikeout rate in our model.

New Pitching Metrics for 2020

We're including a few "new" pitching metrics in the book for the 2020 edition, though unlike last year, these numbers may be a little bit more familiar to those of you who have spent some time investigating baseball statistics.

Fastball Percentage

Our fastball percentage (FB%) statistic measures how frequently a pitcher throws a pitch classified as a "fastball," measured as a percentage of overall pitches thrown. We qualify three types of fastballs:

1. The traditional four-seam fastball;
2. The two-seam fastball or sinker;
3. "Hard cutters," which are pitches that have the movement profile of a cut fastball and are used as the pitcher's primary offering or in place of a more traditional fastball.

For example, a pitcher with a FB% of 67 throws any combination of these three pitches about two-thirds of the time.

Whiff Rate

Everybody loves a swing and a miss, and whiff rate (WHF) measures how frequently pitchers induce a swinging strike. To calculate WHF, we add up all the pitches thrown that ended with a swinging strike, then divide that number by a pitcher's total pitches thrown. Most often, high whiff rates correlate with high strikeout rates (and overall effective pitcher performance).

Called Strike Probability

Called Strike Probability (CSP) is a number that represents the likelihood that all of a pitcher's pitches will be called a strike while controlling for location, pitcher and batter handedness, umpire and count. Here's how it works: on each pitch, our model determines how many times (out of 100) that a similar pitch was called for a strike given those factors mentioned above, and when normalized for each batter's strike zone. Then we average the CSP for all pitches thrown by a pitcher in a season, and that gives us the yearly CSP percentage you see in the stats boxes.

As you might imagine, pitchers with a higher CSP are more likely to work in the zone, where pitchers with a lower CSP are likely locating their pitches outside the normal strike zone, for better or for worse.

Projections

Many of you aren't turning to this book just for a look at what a player has done, but for a look at what a player is going to do: the PECOTA projections. PECOTA, initially developed by Nate Silver (who has moved on to greater fame as a political analyst), consists of three parts:

1. Major-league equivalencies, which use minor-league statistics to project how a player will perform in the major leagues;
2. Baseline forecasts, which use weighted averages and regression to the mean to estimate a player's current true talent level; and
3. Aging curves, which uses the career paths of comparable players to estimate how a player's statistics are likely to change over time.

With all those important things covered, let's take a look at what's in the book this year.

Team Prospectus

Most of this book is composed of team chapters, with one for each of the 30 major-league franchises. On the first page of each chapter, you'll see a box that contains some of the key statistics for each team as well as a very inviting stadium diagram. (You can see an example of this for the Milwaukee Brewers on this very page!)

We start with the team name, their unadjusted 2019 win-loss record, and their divisional ranking. Beneath that are a host of other team statistics. **Pythag** presents an adjusted 2019 winning percentage, calculated by taking runs scored per game (**RS/G**) and runs allowed per game (**RA/G**) for the team, and running them through a version of Bill James' Pythagorean formula that was refined and improved by David Smyth and Brandon Heipp. (The formula is called "Pythagenpat," which is equally fun to type and to say.)

Next up is **DRC+**, described earlier, to indicate the overall hitting ability of the team either above or below league-average. Run prevention on the pitching side is covered by **DRA** (also mentioned earlier) and another metric: Fielding Independent Pitching (**FIP**), which calculates another ERA-like statistic based on strikeouts, walks, and home runs recorded. Defensive Efficiency Rating (**DER**) tells us the percentage of balls in play turned into outs for the team, and is a quick fielding shorthand that rounds out run prevention.

After that, we have several measures related to roster composition, as opposed to on-field performance. **B-Age** and **P-Age** tell us the average age of a team's batters and pitchers, respectively. **Salary** is the combined team payroll for all on-field players, and Doug Pappas' Marginal Dollars per Marginal Win (**M$/MW**) tells us how much money a team spent to earn production above replacement level.

Ending this batch of statistics is the number of disabled list days a team had over the season (**IL Days**) and the amount of salary paid to players on the disabled list (**$ on IL**); this final number is expressed as a percentage of total payroll.

Next to each of these stats, we've listed each team's MLB rank in that category from first to 30th. In this, first always indicates a positive outcome and 30th a negative outcome, except in the case of salary—first is highest.

After the franchise statistics, we share a few items about the team's home ballpark. There's the aforementioned diagram of the park's dimensions (including distances to the outfield wall), a graphic showing the height of the wall from the left-field pole to the right-field pole, and a table showing three-year park factors for the stadium. The park factors are displayed as indexes where 100 is average, 110 means that the park inflates the statistic in question by 10 percent, and 90 means that the park deflates the statistic in question by 10 percent.

On the second page of each team chapter, you'll find three graphs. The first is the **2019 Hit List Ranking**. This shows our Hit List Rank for the team on each day of the 2019 season and is intended to give you a picture of the ups and downs of the team's season. Hit List Rank measures overall team performance and drives the Hit List Power Rankings at the baseballprospectus.com website.

The second graph is **Committed Payroll** and helps you see how the team's payroll has compared to the MLB and divisional average payrolls over time. Payroll figures are current as of January 1, 2020; with so many free agents still unsigned as of this writing, the final 2020 figure will likely be significantly different for many teams. (In the meantime, you can always find the most current data at Baseball Prospectus' Cot's Baseball Contracts page.)

The third graph is **Farm System Ranking** and displays how the Baseball Prospectus prospect team has ranked the organization's farm system since 2007.

After the graphs, we have a **Personnel** section that lists many of the important decision-makers and upper-level field and operations staff members for the franchise, as well as any former Baseball Prospectus staff members who are currently part of the organization. (In very rare circumstances, someone might be on both lists!)

Juan Soto LF

Born: 10/25/98 Age: 21 Bats: L Throws: L
Height: 6'1" Weight: 185 Origin: International Free Agent, 2015

YEAR	TEAM	LVL	AGE	PA	R	2B	3B	HR	RBI	BB	K	SB	CS	AVG/OBP/SLG
2017	NAT	RK	18	27	3	1	1	0	4	2	1	0	0	.320/.370/.440
2017	HAG	A	18	96	15	5	0	3	14	10	8	1	2	.360/.427/.523
2018	HAG	A	19	74	12	5	3	5	24	14	13	2	0	.373/.486/.814
2018	POT	A+	19	73	17	3	1	7	18	11	8	0	1	.371/.466/.790
2018	HAR	AA	19	35	4	2	0	2	10	4	7	1	0	.323/.400/.581
2018	WAS	MLB	19	494	77	25	1	22	70	79	99	5	2	.292/.406/.517
2019	WAS	MLB	20	659	110	32	5	34	110	108	132	12	1	.282/.401/.548
2020	WAS	MLB	21	630	92	30	3	35	102	85	123	5	2	.284/.382/.543

Comparables: Ronald Acuña Jr., Mike Trout, Tony Conigliaro

YEAR	TEAM	LVL	AGE	PA	DRC+	VORP	BABIP	BRR	FRAA	WARP
2017	NAT	RK	18	27	135	1.5	.333	0.0	RF(9): -1.1	0.0
2017	HAG	A	18	96	181	8.0	.373	1.0	RF(19): -1.9, LF(2): -0.3	0.9
2018	HAG	A	19	74	222	14.5	.405	0.3	RF(14): 1.1, CF(2): 0.2	1.2
2018	POT	A+	19	73	260	15.4	.340	1.4	RF(14): 1.0, LF(1): 0.0	1.6
2018	HAR	AA	19	35	113	3.6	.364	0.0	LF(4): 0.6, RF(4): -0.5	0.1
2018	WAS	MLB	19	494	125	40.5	.338	-0.5	LF(114): 2.7	3.0
2019	WAS	MLB	20	659	136	49.0	.312	1.4	LF(150): -0.8	4.9
2020	WAS	MLB	21	630	133	43.6	.310	-0.1	LF 3	4.8

Position Players

After all that information and a thoughtful bylined essay covering each team, we present our player comments. These are also bylined, but due to frequent franchise shifts during the offseason, our bylines are more a rough guide than a perfect accounting of who wrote what.

Each player is listed with the major-league team that employed him as of early January 2020. If a player changed teams after that point via free agency, trade, or any other method, you'll be able to find them in the chapter for their previous squad.

As an example, take a look at the player comment for Nationals outfielder Juan Soto: the stat block that accompanies his written comment is at the top of this page. First we cover biographical information (age is as of June 30, 2020) before moving onto the stats themselves. Our statistic columns include standard identifying information like **YEAR**, **TEAM**, **LVL** (level of affiliated play) and **AGE** before getting into the numbers. Next, we provide raw, untranslated numbers like you might find on the back of your dad's baseball cards: **PA** (plate appearances), **R** (runs), **2B** (doubles), **3B** (triples), **HR** (home runs), **RBI** (runs batted in), **BB** (walks), **K** (strikeouts), **SB** (stolen bases) and **CS** (caught stealing).

Next, we have unadjusted "slash" statistics: **AVG** (batting average), **OBP** (on-base percentage) and **SLG** (slugging percentage). Following the slash line is **DRC+** (Deserved Runs Created Plus), which we described earlier as total offensive expected contribution compared to the league average.

One of our oldest active metrics, **VORP** (Value Over Replacement Player), considers offensive production, position and plate appearances. In essence, it is the number of runs contributed beyond what a replacement-level player at the same position would contribute if given the same percentage of team plate appearances. VORP does not consider the quality of a player's defense.

BABIP (batting average on balls in play) tells us how often a ball in play fell for a hit, and can help us identify whether a batter may have been lucky or not...but note that high BABIPs also tend to follow the great hitters of our time, as well as speedy singles hitters who put the ball on the ground.

The next item is **BRR** (Baserunning Runs), which covers all of a player's baserunning accomplishments including (but not limited to) swiped bags and failed attempts. Next is **FRAA** (Fielding Runs Above Average), which also includes the number of games previously played at each position noted in parentheses. Multi-position players have only their two most frequent positions listed here, but their total FRAA number reflects all positions played.

Our last column here is **WARP** (Wins Above Replacement Player). WARP estimates the total value of a player, which means for hitters it takes into account hitting runs above average (calculated using the DRC+ model), BRR and FRAA. Then, it makes an adjustment for positions played and gives the player a credit for plate appearances based upon the difference between "replacement level"—which is derived from the quality of players added to a team's roster after the start of the season–and the league average.

The final line just below the stats box is **PECOTA** data, which is discussed further in a following section.

Catchers

Catchers are a special breed, and thus they have earned their own separate box which displays some of the defensive metrics that we've built just for them. As an example, let's check out J.T. Realmuto.

The **YEAR** and **TEAM** columns match what you'd find in the other stat box. **P. COUNT** indicates the number of pitches thrown while the catcher was behind the plate, including swinging strikes, fouls and balls in play. **FRM RUNS** is the total run value the catcher provided (or cost) his team by influencing the umpire to call strikes where other catchers did not. **BLK RUNS** expresses the total run value above or below average for the catcher's ability to prevent wild pitches and passed balls. **THRW RUNS** is calculated using a similar model as the previous two statistics, and it measures a catcher's ability to throw out basestealers but also to dissuade them from testing his arm in the first place. It takes into account factors like the pitcher (including his delivery and pickoff move) and baserunner (who could be as fast as Billy Hamilton or as slow as Yonder Alonso). **TOT RUNS** is the sum of all of the previous three statistics.

Justin Verlander   RHP

Born: 02/20/83   Age: 37   Bats: R   Throws: R
Height: 6'5"   Weight: 225   Origin: Round 1, 2004 Draft (#2 overall)

YEAR	TEAM	LVL	AGE	W	L	SV	G	GS	IP	H	HR	BB/9	K/9	K	GB%	BABIP
2017	DET	MLB	34	10	8	0	28	28	172	153	23	3.5	9.2	176	34%	.283
2017	HOU	MLB	34	5	0	0	5	5	34	17	4	1.3	11.4	43	32%	.194
2018	HOU	MLB	35	16	9	0	34	34	214	156	28	1.6	12.2	290	31%	.272
2019	HOU	MLB	36	21	6	0	34	34	223	137	36	1.7	12.1	300	36%	.219
2020	HOU	MLB	37	15	6	0	29	29	184	138	28	2.3	12.1	248	35%	.274

Comparables: Zack Greinke, A.J. Burnett, Aníbal Sánchez

YEAR	TEAM	LVL	AGE	WHIP	ERA	DRA	WARP	MPH	FB%	WHF	CSP
2017	DET	MLB	34	1.28	3.82	4.03	3.0	97.7	58	11	47.8
2017	HOU	MLB	34	0.65	1.06	3.08	0.9	97.5	59.6	15.1	49.9
2018	HOU	MLB	35	0.90	2.52	2.33	7.3	97.5	61.2	16.2	51.6
2019	HOU	MLB	36	0.80	2.58	2.51	7.9	96.8	49.9	17.5	48.3
2020	HOU	MLB	37	1.01	2.75	2.95	5.3	95.8	54.6	15.1	48.2

Pitchers

Let's give our pitchers a turn, using 2019 AL Cy Young winner Justin Verlander as our example. Take a look at his stat block: the first line and the **YEAR, TEAM, LVL** and **AGE** columns are the same as in the position player example earlier.

Here too, we have a series of columns that display raw, unadjusted statistics compiled by the pitcher over the course of a season: **W** (wins), **L** (losses), **SV** (saves), **G** (games pitched), **GS** (games started), **IP** (innings pitched), **H** (hits allowed) and **HR** (home runs allowed). Next we have two statistics that are rates: **BB/9** (walks per nine innings) and **K/9** (strikeouts per nine innings), before returning to the unadjusted K (strikeouts).

Next up is **GB%** (ground ball percentage), which is the percentage of all batted balls that were hit on the ground, including both outs and hits. Remember, this is based on observational data and subject to human error, so please approach this with a healthy dose of skepticism.

BABIP (batting average on balls in play) is calculated using the same methodology as it is for position players, but it often tells us more about a pitcher than it does a hitter. With pitchers, a high BABIP is often due to poor defense or bad luck, and can often be an indicator of potential rebound, and a low BABIP may be cause to expect performance regression. (A typical league-average BABIP is close to .290-.300.)

Pittsburgh Pirates 2020

The metrics **WHIP** (walks plus hits per inning pitched) and **ERA** (earned run average) are old standbys: WHIP measures walks and hits allowed on a per-inning basis, while ERA measures earned runs on a nine-inning basis. Neither of these stats are translated or adjusted.

DRA (Deserved Run Average) was described at length earlier, and measures how many runs the pitcher "deserved" to allow per nine innings. Please note that since we lack all the data points that would make for a "real" DRA for minor-league events, the DRA displayed for minor league partial-seasons is based off of different data. (That data is a modified version of our cFIP metric, which you can find more information about on our website.)

Just like with hitters, **WARP** (Wins Above Replacement Player) is a total value metric that puts pitchers of all stripes on the same scale as position players. We use DRA as the primary input for our calculation of WARP. You might notice that relief pitchers (due to their limited innings) may have a lower WARP than you were expecting or than you might see in other WARP-like metrics. WARP does not take leverage into account, just the actions a pitcher performs and the expected value of those actions…which ends up judging high-leverage relief pitchers differently than you might imagine given their prestige and market value.

MPH gives you the pitcher's 95th percentile velocity for the noted season, in order to give you an idea of what the *peak* fastball velocity a pitcher possesses. Since this comes from our pitch-tracking data, it is not publicly available for minor-league pitchers.

Finally, we display the three new pitching metrics we described earlier. **FB%** (fastball percentage) gives you the percentage of fastballs thrown out of all pitches. **WHF** (whiff rate) tells you the percentage of swinging strikes induced out of all pitches. **CSP** (called strike probability) expresses the likelihood of all pitches thrown to result in a called strike, after controlling for factors like handedness, umpire, pitch type, count and location.

PECOTA

All players have PECOTA projections for 2020, as well as a set of other numbers that describe the performance of comparable players according to PECOTA. All projections for 2020 are for the player at the date we went to press in early January and are projected into the league and park context as indicated by the team abbreviation. (Note that players at very low levels of the minors are too unpredictable to assess using these numbers.) All PECOTA projected statistics represent a player's projected major-league performance.

Below the projections are the player's three highest-scoring comparable players as determined by PECOTA. All comparables represent a snapshot of how the listed player was performing at the same age as the current player, so if a

23-year-old pitcher is compared to Bartolo Colón, he's actually being compared to a 23-year-old Colón, not the version that pitched for the Rangers in 2018, nor to Colón's career as a whole.

A few points about pitcher projections. First, we aren't yet projecting peak velocity, so that column will be blank in the PECOTA lines. Second, projecting DRA is trickier than evaluating past performance, because it is unclear how deserving each pitcher will be of his anticipated outcomes. However, we know that another DRA-related statistic–contextual FIP or cFIP–estimates future run scoring very well. So for PECOTA, the projected DRA figures you see are based on the past cFIPs generated by the pitcher and comparable players over time, along with the other factors described above.

Lineouts

In each chapter's Lineouts section, you'll find abbreviated text comments, as well as all the same information you'd find in our full player comments. The only difference is that we limit the stats boxes in this section to only including the 2019 information for each player.

Managers

After all those wonderful team chapters, we've got statistics for each big-league manager, all of whom are organized by alphabetical order. Here you'll find a block including an extraordinary amount of information collected from each manager's entire career. For more information on the acronyms and what they mean, please visit the Glossary at www.baseballprospectus.com.

There is one important metric that we'd like to call attention to, and you'll find it next to each manager's name: **wRM+** (weighted reliever management plus). Developed by Rob Arthur and Rian Watt, wRM+ investigates how good a manager is at using their best relievers during the moments of highest leverage, using both our proprietary DRA metric as well as Leverage Index. wRM+ is scaled to a league average of 100, and a wRM+ of 105 indicates that relievers were used approximately five percent "better" than average. On the other hand, a wRM+ of 95 would tell us the team used its relievers five percent "worse" than the average team.

While wRM+ does not have an extremely strong correlation with a manager, it is statistically significant; this means that a manager is not *entirely* responsible for a team's wRM+, but does have some effect on that number.

PECOTA Leaderboards

If you're familiar with PECOTA, then you'll have noticed that the projection system often appears bullish on players coming off a bad year and bearish on players coming off a good year. (This is because the system weights several previous seasons, not just the most recent one.) In addition, we publish the 50th

Pittsburgh Pirates 2020

percentile projections for each player–which is smack in the middle of the range of projected production—which tends to mean PECOTA stat lines don't often have extreme results like 40 home runs or 250 strikeouts in a given season. In essence, PECOTA doesn't project very many extreme seasons.

At the end of the book, we've ranked the top players at each position based on their PECOTA projections. This might help you visualize just how a given player's projection compares to that of their peers, so that even if a dramatic stat line isn't projected, you can still imagine how they stack up against the rest of the league.

Part 1: Team Analysis

Pittsburgh Pirates: Where Are You Going, Where Have You Been?

Brian Duricy, Ben Spanier and Matthew Trueblood

2019: What Went Right

After the first 20 games of the season, the Pirates found themselves tied for the division lead. Prior to the season, PECOTA saw Pittsburgh as a slightly below-.500 team; if everything went their way, contending for the second Wild Card spot would still be surprising while not out of the realm of possibility. Chris Archer, Jameson Taillon, and Joe Musgrove had 13 starts combined in which each pitched to or above their expectations from the year prior. Only two of the eight losses in those first 20 games were by more than two runs. They'd played six extra-innings games by this point, winning the last four. If it was hard to imagine the Pirates as a division contender, one could at least conceive of them as potential buyers at the trade deadline.

Such fantasies proved to be fleeting. Though the Pirates were .500 at the close of May, they began June 2-10 and were already nine games out of first place by the middle of the month. Nevertheless, the season did have a handful of performances that Pittsburgh can build off of in 2020. Josh Bell transformed from a league-average hitter in his first three seasons into one of the best offensive players in the majors, regularly hitting fly balls that would be out of most parks. He closed out May with a 1.109 OPS, then cooled off dramatically, hitting only .232/.342/.476 the rest of the way. Nonetheless, his season can still be rated a success.

Bryan Reynolds' expectations-exceeding performance was surely helped by a .387 BABIP—though DRC+ still finds him solidly above-average on the year. The pitching staff was better than expected as a whole by DRA-. Unfortunately, that still meant they were 10th in the NL and last in their division. Joe Musgrove continued to improve and was easily the best starting pitcher on the team.

Elsewhere, Adam Frazier continued being a reliable hitter for average. Kevin Newman's first full season showed him to be someone the Pirates can trust as their leadoff hitter. Starling Marte tied his career high in WARP, which if it accomplished nothing else finally made him attractive enough to be profitably traded for two good prospects and international bonus money. Jacob Stallings has been a top-10 defensive catcher while displaying a nearly league-average bat. The above performances combined with the relative youth of most of these players give Pittsburgh an offensive foundation that's a star (or two) away from being competitive in the NL Central.

2019: What Went Wrong

If there's something worse than FOMO, Fear Of Missing Out, it's YADMO, You Actually Did Miss Out. The performances of Gerrit Cole, Austin Meadows, Tyler Glasnow, and, in the future, Shane Baz will continue to haunt the Pirates and Pirates fans for years. With Meadows, the Pirates would have had a second Josh Bell-level season. The value of an ace like Gerrit Cole is self-explanatory, to say nothing of how his addition to the rotation would have pushed Musgrove or Archer down to third starter, making a hypothetical potential playoff rotation that much more effective.

The key word there, of course, being hypothetical. Archer's second season in Pittsburgh was the worst of his career. There was a season-long drop in fastball velocity, but the most concerning change was his degraded control. Archer was never elite in terms of limiting walks, but a rate of 4.1 per nine was nearly a walk higher than his second-highest ratio in a full season. His career-worst home-run rate and being in the bottom seven percent of the league in barrel percentage contributed to the carnage as well. Allowing more home runs is at least somewhat attributable to the current inflationary era but getting ahead in counts again is a potential fix over which Archer has more control.

Jameson Taillon missed nearly the entirety of 2019 and will be out for all of 2020 following a second Tommy John surgery. He was one of the best pitchers in the majors in 2018 and was hoped to make yet another considerable improvement over the prior year. Mitch Keller made his major-league debut with high expectations, and while DRA- has him at over 10 percent better than league-average, no advanced metric will make a 7.12 ERA over 11 starts seem any less bad for pitcher and team alike. Infielder Cole Tucker also debuted but failed to hit, posting a 62 DRC+ and a .626 OPS. The Pirates bungled its response to Francisco Cervelli's many concussion issues prior to releasing him to risk his brain in pursuit of a Braves pennant.

Finally, Felipe Vázquez's issues transcend baseball. As far as is known at this writing he was the best of relief pitchers and the worst of human beings. There are fans (and/or former members of the Houston front office) who would make a deal with the Devil to win a championship, but no transient moment of celebration is worth the permanent stain of that association. It has been a long, low time for the Pirates since 1979, but it is to be appreciated that whenever the drought finally ends, Vázquez will not be a part of it. When a player in his prime suffers a career-ending injury it is normally an occasion for mourning, but in this case mourning should be reserved for Vázquez's victim. The Pirates will find another good closer in time.

In the first half, the Pirates were just under .500 (44-45). Their second-half winning percentage was just .342, equivalent to a 55-107 record over a full season. With most of the team's top prospects entering the season now in Pittsburgh, improvements will have to arrive externally. Luckily, PNC Park has a truly unbeatable view—if only one lifts one's eyes from the field. —*Brian Duricy*

Prospect Outlook

The Pirates farm system always seems to reflect water-treading of the club generally, never ranking at the top of the heap but never devoid of talent either. This era of Pirates' prospects is no different, but they have managed to graduate only a couple productive bats over the last couple years. Josh Bell and Bryan Reynolds would qualify (though Bell was drafted in 2011 and Reynolds was acquired in the McCutchen trade), but the Buccos will need a lot more where that came from if they are going to compete on their at least partially self-imposed shoestring budget.

Fortunately, there are a few promising hitters in the minors, some closer to impact than others. Third baseman **Ke'Bryan Hayes** should be the next man up. He had a solid age-22 season at Triple-A Indianapolis. He is a good defender and shows gap power and a good approach at the plate; he's a near slam dunk to be a solid player at the big-league level. Whether he'll be much more than solid is an open question, as he still hasn't translated his bat speed into home-run power even as the level exploded with tens of springy baseballs a night flying over fences. The most intriguing prospect in the organization is probably **Oneil Cruz**, a 6-foot-6 shortstop who cracked Double-A Altoona at the age of 20. Most reports insist he can play shortstop despite his frame. Even if he doesn't, he's a pretty good hitter with some big left-handed power potential. High-A Bradenton boasted a pair of intriguing outfield prospects in **Travis Swaggerty** and **Cal Mitchell**, the former an athlete with big tools and the latter more of a pure hitter.

The reinforcements are less clear on the pitching side. Mitch Keller debuted this year and had it rough, though his peripherals indicate that he should be fine going forward. Most of the system pitching talent, such as it is, is in the low minors. **Luis Escobar** had a solid campaign at Indianapolis and should help in the bullpen soon, but the rest of the names are years away. –*Ben Spanier*

2020 Outlook

Change was far overdue on the banks of the Allegheny, and it finally came. Clint Hurdle, Ray Searage and Neal Huntington probably should have been fired after 2017, and clearly needed to go after 2018. Finally, the team (spurred by a firing even further up the ladder, as team president Frank Coonelly was let go as well) took action. The organization needs smarter, more modern, less testosterone-fueled player-development practices. It needs clearer, more accountable, less testosterone-fueled leadership. It needs a coherent plan and people with the patience and intellect to execute it. Ben Cherington and Derek Shelton are, in that sense, a good start.

Cherington is famous for big-picture, future-focused thinking, and given the state of the team he inherited, it's no surprise that he steered them into a full-fledged rebuild. His patience paid off in a solid return for Starling Marte, though if not for ownership's constant mandate that no dollar be spent without playoff tickets being printed, the team might have pondered keeping Marte. Knowing what he was brought in to do, however, Cherington waited out the market and made the best possible move. He also made small supplemental moves, partially replacing Marte by signing Guillermo Heredia for the outfield and increasing the fluidity of a crowded middle infield by inking J.T. Riddle. It's going to be a forgettable year or two, but the Pirates got some of the messiest and most painful items on their turnaround to-do list done this offseason. —*Matthew Trueblood*

Performance Graphs

2019 Hit List Ranking

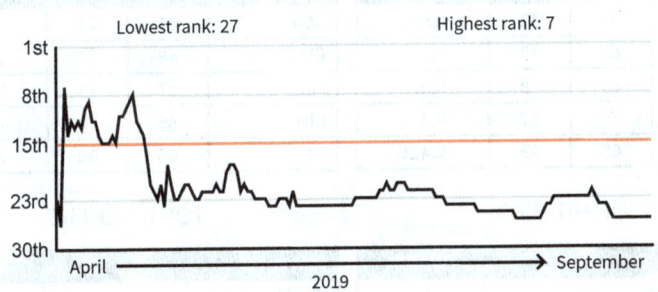

Committed Payroll (in millions)

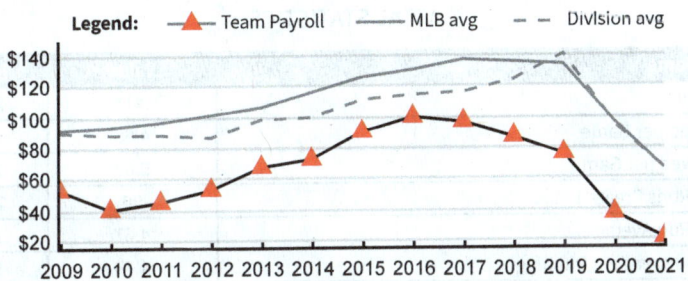

Farm System Ranking

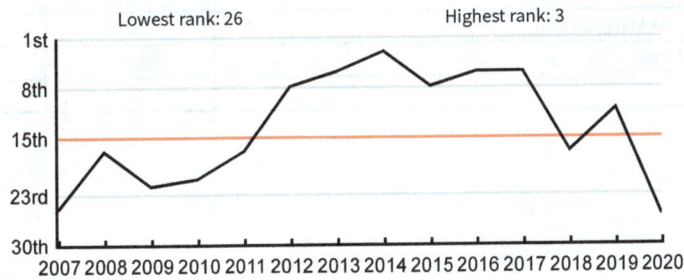

2019 Team Performance

ACTUAL STANDINGS

Team	W	L	Pct
SLN	91	71	0.562
MIL	89	73	0.549
CHN	84	78	0.519
CIN	75	87	0.463
PIT	**69**	**93**	**0.426**

THIRD-ORDER STANDINGS

Team	W	L	Pct
SLN	91	71	0.564
CHN	88	74	0.543
MIL	87	75	0.535
CIN	86	76	0.534
PIT	**66**	**96**	**0.407**

TOP HITTERS

Player	WARP
Starling Marte	3.4
Kevin Newman	2.8
Jacob Stallings	2.3

TOP PITCHERS

Player	WARP
Joe Musgrove	4.0
Felipe Vázquez	2.0
Chris Archer	1.8

VITAL STATISTICS

Statistic Name	Value	Rank
Pythagenpat	.411	26th
Runs Scored per Game	4.68	20th
Runs Allowed per Game	5.62	27th
Deserved Runs Created Plus	90	24th
Deserved Run Average	4.67	12th
Fielding Independent Pitching	4.73	19th
Defensive Efficiency Rating	.685	29th
Batter Age	27.4	6th
Pitcher Age	27.1	5th
Salary	$74.8M	28th
Marginal $ per Marginal Win	$3.0M	23rd
Injured List Days	2091	29th
$ on IL	35%	30th

2020 Team Projections

PROJECTED STANDINGS

Team	W	L	Pct	+/-
CIN	86.1	75.9	0.531	11
CHN	84.5	77.5	0.522	0
SLN	80.3	81.7	0.496	-11
MIL	79.4	82.6	0.490	-10
PIT	**70.3**	**91.7**	**0.434**	**1**

TOP PROJECTED HITTERS

Player	WARP
Bryan Reynolds	2.8
Josh Bell	2.1
Adam Frazier	1.5

TOP PROJECTED PITCHERS

Player	WARP
Joe Musgrove	2.5
Chris Archer	2.2
Trevor Williams	1.3

FARM SYSTEM REPORT

Top Prospect	Number of Top 101 Prospects
Mitch Keller, #53	3

KEY DEDUCTIONS

Player	WARP
Starling Marte	3.4
Francisco Liriano	0.0
Parker Markel	-0.2
Dario Agrazal	-0.5

KEY ADDITIONS

Player	WARP
Oneil Cruz	0.5
Guillermo Heredia	0.5
Will Craig	0.4
Luke Maile	0.3
Jarrod Dyson	0.2
Ke'Bryan Hayes	0.1
John Ryan Murphy	0.1
Robbie Erlin	0.1
Sam Howard	0.1
Cody Ponce	0.0

Team Personnel

President
Travis Williams

General Manager
Ben Cherington

Assistant General Manager
Kevan Graves

Assistant General Manager
Steve Sanders

Manager
Derek Shelton

BP Alumni
Dan Fox
Grant Jones

PNC Park Stats

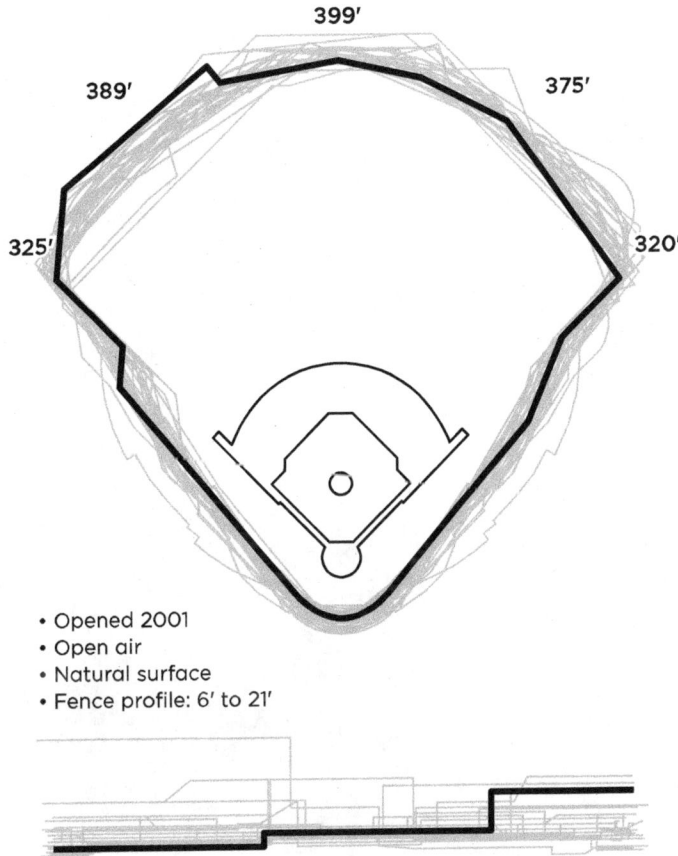

- Opened 2001
- Open air
- Natural surface
- Fence profile: 6' to 21'

Three-Year Park Factors

Runs	Runs/RH	Runs/LH	HR/RH	HR/LH
96	96	96	89	98

Pirates Team Analysis

In the photo, Clint Hurdle is free. He smiles. He's dressed like a man of a certain age who wants to head out and have a little *fun*—slip-on shoes, button-down in a joyful plaid, glasses loose around his neck—and he rides on a cart driven by someone else. Getty Images provides context ("Former Pittsburgh Pirates manager Clint Hurdle leaves the clubhouse after being relieved of managerial duties…") but the picture doesn't need that. Hurdle's smile does it all.

The photo was taken about two hours before the start of Game 162, which is an odd time to be fired, given its proximity to the more reasonable alternatives of the night before or morning after or even just later that day. But to fire Hurdle at one of those times would have indicated a certain organizational competency, and these were the 2019 Pirates, so instead, it went like this. There was a report that Hurdle would stay in the job that he was under contract to do for two more years; Hurdle declared his desire to stay; the team said that there was no official decision; a few days passed with no clarity. Hurdle came to the stadium for Game 162. He held court with the media to discuss his plans for the future of the club. And then he was fired.

Moves like these are typically assessed on a binary. A firing feels certain or it feels like a shock. It is good or it is bad. There is not much gray area; by the time that a team has arrived at any discussion of these questions, much of the nuance has been beaten out of the situation, and the public isn't privy to detail that could add another dimension. These are definitive moves described in terms to match.

Which made the Pirates' dismissals—Hurdle, and then all the rest—unusual.

The Pirates did not come down on these binary lines. Instead, the team created a weird little place to live in between them. The moves felt certain—how could they *not*, after this season?—yet they were timed and handled in such a way that they came across in the moment as minor shocks. They were collectively necessary but with individually conflicted definitions of "need." They led to a different staff for a club that may not feel so very different at all. The 2020 Pirates now have as clean a slate as a team could ever ask for. They've torn out the roots of their issues from 2019, the managerial staff, the front office, all of it. But their path to this fresh start was so torturous and ill-timed and simply *weird* that the fresh start itself may not matter much at all.

If you were trying to read this situation logically, Hurdle's dismissal communicated a particular set of priorities. *This was The Problem*, it said. He was fired by himself, without his coaches, without anyone from the front office.

So if you were in search of reason—if you wanted to believe that there was a process, that the club had been evaluated holistically, that the motivation had been to locate the source of the issue here—Hurdle's departure looked like a reflection of the team's values. Just read the statement that announced it: "As an organization," GM Neal Huntington wrote, "we believe it was time for a managerial change to introduce a new voice and new leadership inside the clubhouse." It was not that he neatly placed himself inside the organizational "we" and outside the need for "new leadership"; it was that he was the one to make this statement in the first place. Huntington had signed his contract extension at the same time as Hurdle, back in 2017, and he trusted that he would see out his term—with good reason. Owner Bob Nutting issued his own statement: Huntington would not be fired. ("I strongly believe Neal Huntington and the leadership team that he has assembled are the right people...," a vote of confidence across the board.) There was no official word about other moves, not later that day, or the next one, or the next. It was just Hurdle.

If you were trying to read this situation logically, this demonstrated the team's assessment of The Problem. It was the manager, not the general manager, not his coaches. It was leadership. It was morale; it was the clubhouse fights and the other fights and the full-on second-half meltdown. This was a curiously partial read of the situation but not an incorrect one. (Those *were* problems, certainly, but they were not the only ones and arguably not close to the most pressing ones.) Yet there were no other moves for almost a week, and so if you were trying to read this situation logically, the conclusion stood: The Pirates had felt that Hurdle was the central source of the issue.

If you were trying to read this situation logically, if you really tried, you could find a coherent statement here. This was a team that seemed to believe in its process. It seemed to believe in its strategy and its roster construction and its organizational philosophy. Should it? That was almost beside the point. There was a direction, if (very) arguably not the most rational direction. The Pirates had delivered a clear affirmation of their commitment to Huntington & Co. They seemed to be firm; they knew what they valued and were not stuck on any hypothetical visions of Gerrit Cole and Tyler Glasnow. This was the size and substance of the problem, Pittsburgh said: Hurdle. They'd made a statement there. You could carry the coherence of that statement as they went on to fire pitching coach Ray Searage and bench coach Tim Prince—a little unusual that they hadn't done it with or immediately after Hurdle, but not so unusual, really—and as they went on to "part ways" with team president Frank Coonelly, because how do you draw lines around the exact area of responsibility of the team president, anyway? The statement held. You could find extreme fault with the foundational beliefs of this statement, obviously. But you could see its internal coherence. Until you couldn't.

If you were trying to read this situation logically, on October 28, you had to stop trying. It was three days after the Red Sox, the only team with a vacancy at GM, had announced that they'd found their man after more than a month of searching. It was one day after Cole had thrown a phenomenal start in Game 5 of the World Series, his last appearance before he'd officially become the best pitcher in the history of free agency. And it was, of course, the day that the Pirates fired Neal Huntington.

It was not that it was illogical to fire him. (It can very easily be argued that the only logical choice was to fire him.) It was that to fire him *then* threw the team's entire endeavor into question. The coherence of the Pirates' initial statements broke. If Huntington had deserved a public vote of confidence on September 29, what changed in the period of relative inactivity that ran to his last day on October 28? If Huntington had been the one to fire Hurdle, what did this mean about his successor? (When Huntington was dismissed, most teams had already filled their managerial vacancies; the Angels, Cubs, Phillies and Padres were done, and within the week, they'd be joined by the Royals and Mets. The Pirates now had yet to even decide who would be in a position to hire for them, let alone who they'd hire.) What did this say about how the team saw its own situation? There was no good answer to any of these. The most generous reading of the situation was that the Pirates had clumsily stumbled through making the right moves in the wrong way at inconvenient times. A less generous reading was…far less generous.

This gave a wildly different view of The Problem. It was the leadership, it was the strategy, it was the roster, it was the vision. It required firing Hurdle, Searage, Prince, Coonelly, Huntington. The Problem was everything. Which—obviously. Obviously. The Problem had quite clearly been all of this all along. And the fact that it had ever been positioned as anything else demonstrated its own problem: *How could you fail to recognize The Problem?*

⚾ ⚾ ⚾

The Pirates went on to make a series of smart hires. (On a timeline that involved naming a manager almost a full month after the last one had been announced, and a GM weeks after the conclusion of the GM Meetings, but that's neither here nor there.) Derek Shelton and Ben Cherington and the rest are well-positioned to make this team better. But in the context of how these hires were made, it feels relevant to look at who has stayed in place, rather than who has moved. And there is only one truly notable person who has stayed in place, and, of course, he's the only one who cannot easily be removed: Nutting, who oversaw all of this as chairman of the board, and who failed to recognize The Problem. Inasmuch as The Problem is everything, The Problem is Nutting. That will not be different.

It's not that the Pirates can't succeed under Nutting; they have, obviously, and they very well may do it again, maybe even this season. But with Nutting, their window for success is smaller and the conditions are narrower and it all demands far more delicate choreography than is the case for most teams. That's a matter of money, of course, but also of basic sense. It's one thing to have the Pirates' chronically low payroll. It's another to react to this season with this autumn, executed with such staggeringly poor timing and planning.

You should not try to read these situations logically. You can't. Who could?

⚾ ⚾ ⚾

In his media session before Game 162, when he still believed that he would not be fired, Hurdle said the typical things about believing in this group of men and being ready to put in the work for next season, and he also said this:

"I continue to hold fast when I evaluate things. I look at honest, realistic information, and then guarded and guided optimism that is fueled by belief, not hope."

Now, of course, Hurdle's views on the team are of limited use. But his comment here still feels relevant; even after the turmoil of the offseason, this read on the situation is sharp enough to cut through. It does not look like much, and, really, it's an increasingly common sentiment, in baseball and elsewhere. But under its drab cover of practicality, its stilted corporate cold, the statement's truth sits clear and shrill: *Hope has no place here.* It does not say that the situation is hopeless, of course, *that* would be bad. It simply notes that hope does not seem to be a useful instrument in this context.

This Pirates team is not that Pirates team. It's different. But if you look at honest, realistic information, and then guarded and guided optimism that is fueled by belief—if you try to read the situation logically—it could be fair to conclude, like Hurdle, that hope has no place here.

—*Emma Baccellieri is a staff writer at Sports Illustrated.*

Part 2: Player Analysis

PLAYER COMMENTS WITH GRAPHS

Josh Bell 1B
Born: 08/14/92 Age: 27 Bats: B Throws: R
Height: 6'4" Weight: 240 Origin: Round 2, 2011 Draft (#61 overall)

YEAR	TEAM	LVL	AGE	PA	R	2B	3B	HR	RBI	BB	K	SB	CS	AVG/OBP/SLG
2017	PIT	MLB	24	620	75	26	6	26	90	66	117	2	4	.255/.334/.466
2018	PIT	MLB	25	583	74	31	4	12	62	77	104	2	5	.261/.357/.411
2019	PIT	MLB	26	613	94	37	3	37	116	74	118	0	1	.277/.367/.569
2020	PIT	MLB	27	630	81	33	4	29	91	74	119	4	3	.258/.348/.487

Comparables: Justin Smoak, Steve Bilko, Freddie Freeman

Not only did Bell lead switch-hitters in home runs last year, his 37 dingers were most by a Bucco since Brian Giles hit 38 in 2002. He did all this with a better-than-average strikeout rate and a scant amount of lineup help. Though they feel as outdated as the rotary phone or Adobe Flash, burly first-base-only swatsmen might be making a comeback. (It's also possible it's just another level of irony foisted upon baseball.) Their return makes sense, what with everybody just swinging as hard as they can, positional flexibility be danged. Perhaps Bell and his counterparts will bring us back to the golden days, when the tragically slow were permitted to forego "defense" in favor of making small talk with the baserunner (now *those* were the original DMs). Of course, the other part of that social contract entails going yicketty with regularity. Bell, for his part, should have no problem upholding it.

YEAR	TEAM	LVL	AGE	PA	DRC+	VORP	BABIP	BRR	FRAA	WARP
2017	PIT	MLB	24	620	108	18.3	.278	-3.7	1B(147): -6.5	0.5
2018	PIT	MLB	25	583	101	19.7	.305	-0.8	1B(137): -6.8	0.1
2019	PIT	MLB	26	613	131	34.4	.288	-3.1	1B(134): -11.1	2.0
2020	PIT	MLB	27	630	119	26.5	.281	-1.6	1B -6	2.1

Josh Bell, continued

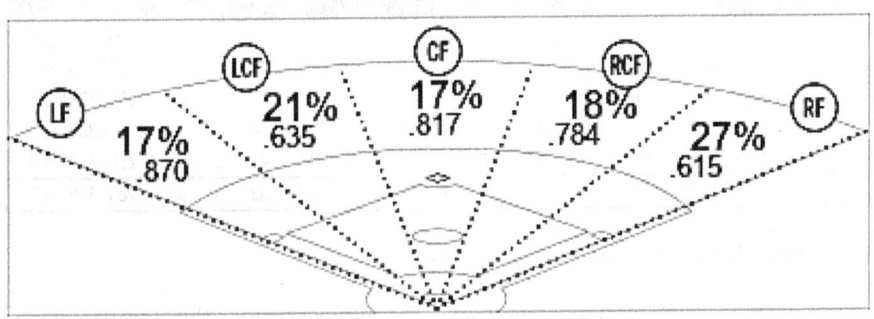

Batted Ball Distribution

Strike Zone vs LHP   **Strike Zone vs RHP**

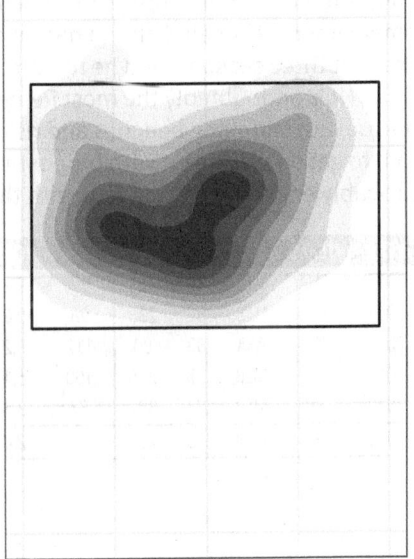

Pittsburgh Pirates 2020

Melky Cabrera   RF
Born: 08/11/84   Age: 35   Bats: B   Throws: L
Height: 5'10"   Weight: 210   Origin: International Free Agent, 2001

YEAR	TEAM	LVL	AGE	PA	R	2B	3B	HR	RBI	BB	K	SB	CS	AVG/OBP/SLG
2017	CHA	MLB	32	428	54	17	0	13	56	25	52	0	0	.295/.336/.436
2017	KCA	MLB	32	238	24	13	2	4	29	11	22	1	2	.269/.303/.399
2018	COH	AAA	33	80	7	6	1	0	8	2	10	2	0	.321/.338/.423
2018	CLE	MLB	33	278	28	17	0	6	39	20	38	1	1	.280/.335/.420
2019	PIT	MLB	34	397	43	22	1	7	47	17	41	2	0	.280/.313/.399
2020	PIT	MLB	35	251	23	13	1	5	26	14	33	1	0	.264/.308/.389

Comparables: Mark Kotsay, Darin Erstad, Johnny Damon

These days, the Melkman delivers to only the midwest. Since the start of the 2015 season, he's played for four teams, and all of them have been housed in a Central division. So far as we know, there's no rhyme or reason to Cabrera's employment choices. Maybe he just likes America's heartland? Or maybe the constant mediocrity of the AL Central has lent itself to his continued employment. After all, Cabrera has finished below replacement level in two of the past three seasons, and he has amassed all of 1.5 wins since the start of 2015. He's undoubtedly the most Remember Some Guys player left in the league. But shrinking benches and rising standards means it's about time for him to get on getting on with his post-playing days. First, however, he'll probably enjoy a year-long tour with the Tigers.

YEAR	TEAM	LVL	AGE	PA	DRC+	VORP	BABIP	BRR	FRAA	WARP
2017	CHA	MLB	32	428	97	9.2	.310	-2.2	LF(92): -5.7	0.1
2017	KCA	MLB	32	238	98	0.0	.280	0.6	RF(46): -6.3, LF(12): -0.6	-0.2
2018	COH	AAA	33	80	112	1.2	.368	-1.0	RF(10): 0.4, LF(6): 0.9	0.3
2018	CLE	MLB	33	278	100	6.1	.303	-0.4	RF(68): 1.7, LF(4): 0.0	0.7
2019	PIT	MLB	34	397	87	3.5	.300	-2.0	RF(74): -5.8, LF(24): -2.8	-0.7
2020	PIT	MLB	35	251	84	2.4	.290	-0.5	RF -3, LF -1	-0.2

Melky Cabrera, continued

Batted Ball Distribution

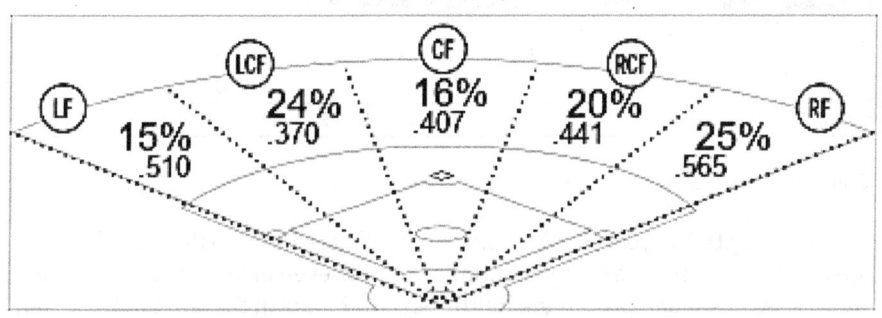

Strike Zone vs LHP **Strike Zone vs RHP**

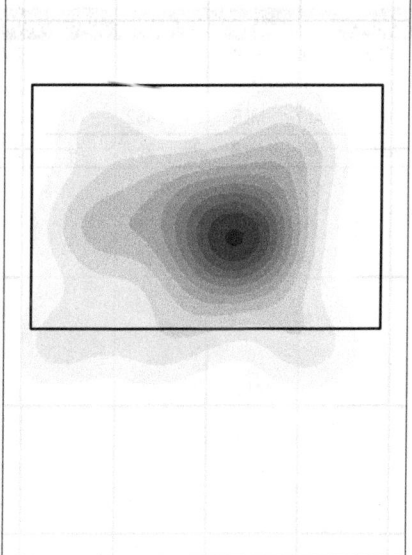

Pittsburgh Pirates 2020

Jarrod Dyson CF

Born: 08/15/84 Age: 35 Bats: L Throws: R
Height: 5'10" Weight: 165 Origin: Round 50, 2006 Draft (#1475 overall)

YEAR	TEAM	LVL	AGE	PA	R	2B	3B	HR	RBI	BB	K	SB	CS	AVG/OBP/SLG
2017	SEA	MLB	32	390	56	13	3	5	30	28	55	28	7	.251/.324/.350
2018	ARI	MLB	33	237	29	4	2	2	12	27	34	16	3	.189/.282/.257
2019	ARI	MLB	34	452	65	11	2	7	27	47	86	30	4	.230/.313/.320
2020	ARI	MLB	35	251	24	9	2	3	22	22	49	17	4	.233/.308/.340

Comparables: John Moses, Mookie Wilson, Omar Moreno

Dyson has lasted 10 years in the majors for two incredibly obvious reasons: speed and defense. The former continued to hold even in his age-34 season, as he stole 30 bases and posted the fourth-best BRR mark in the league. The latter, though, took a step back. Dyson's skill set is well suited for a fourth outfielder, but if his defense continues to decline as he enters his mid-30s, so too will his opportunities for work.

YEAR	TEAM	LVL	AGE	PA	DRC+	VORP	BABIP	BRR	FRAA	WARP
2017	SEA	MLB	32	390	80	2.7	.285	0.0	CF(96): 5.6, LF(12): 3.2	1.2
2018	ARI	MLB	33	237	70	-3.6	.216	2.6	CF(41): 3.3, RF(18): 0.0	0.6
2019	ARI	MLB	34	452	77	2.0	.275	6.3	CF(103): -3.7, RF(21): 4.0	0.8
2020	ARI	MLB	35	251	74	0.7	.283	1.2	CF 1, RF 0	0.1

Jarrod Dyson, continued

Batted Ball Distribution

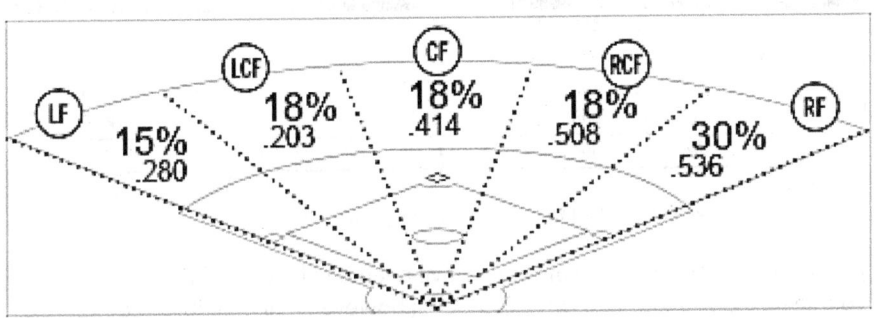

Strike Zone vs LHP   **Strike Zone vs RHP**

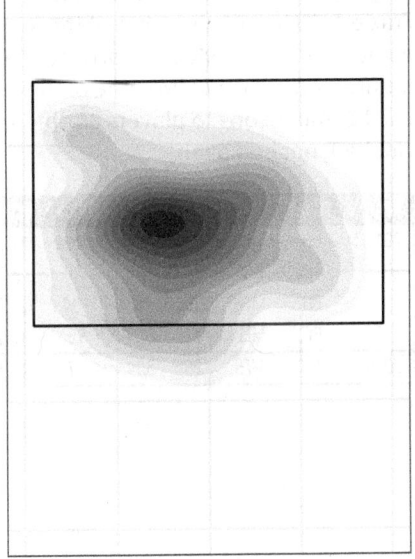

Adam Frazier 2B

Born: 12/14/91   Age: 28   Bats: L   Throws: R
Height: 5'10"   Weight: 180   Origin: Round 6, 2013 Draft (#179 overall)

YEAR	TEAM	LVL	AGE	PA	R	2B	3B	HR	RBI	BB	K	SB	CS	AVG/OBP/SLG
2017	PIT	MLB	25	454	55	20	6	6	53	36	57	9	5	.276/.344/.399
2018	IND	AAA	26	137	10	5	2	0	18	11	20	1	3	.223/.289/.298
2018	PIT	MLB	26	352	52	23	2	10	35	29	53	1	3	.277/.342/.456
2019	PIT	MLB	27	608	80	33	7	10	50	40	75	5	5	.278/.336/.417
2020	PIT	MLB	28	504	49	26	4	9	51	36	72	9	6	.260/.321/.391

Comparables: Whitey Lockman, Carl Yastrzemski, Chris Coghlan

Is Frazier what David Eckstein would have been had he played in this era? Of course not, Eckstein is his own gritty deity; however, if he had injected the (completely legal) wood nymph serum that caused the home-run spike, then he might have been able to crush 10 dingers a year as well. Frazier is the kind of undersized contact hitter who bats leadoff and has just enough power to justify playing exclusively second base rather than deploying as a utility type. Five of Frazier's 10 home runs were of the leadoff variety, so he left the park to begin a game as often as Kyle Schwarber did. For evidence concerning Frazier's protean nature, consider that he's one of the few (and presumably the proud) who can elicit comparisons to players as different as David Eckstein and Kyle Schwarber. Not bad, not bad at all.

YEAR	TEAM	LVL	AGE	PA	DRC+	VORP	BABIP	BRR	FRAA	WARP
2017	PIT	MLB	25	454	96	17.3	.306	1.3	LF(52): 2.8, 2B(42): -2.6	1.1
2018	IND	AAA	26	137	71	-2.3	.262	-0.9	2B(17): 0.0, RF(7): -0.6	-0.2
2018	PIT	MLB	26	352	104	21.7	.305	1.7	2B(55): 2.5, LF(14): 0.7	1.6
2019	PIT	MLB	27	608	95	16.2	.306	1.0	2B(142): -6.4	1.1
2020	PIT	MLB	28	504	91	15.5	.291	1.2	2B -2	1.4

Adam Frazier, continued

Batted Ball Distribution

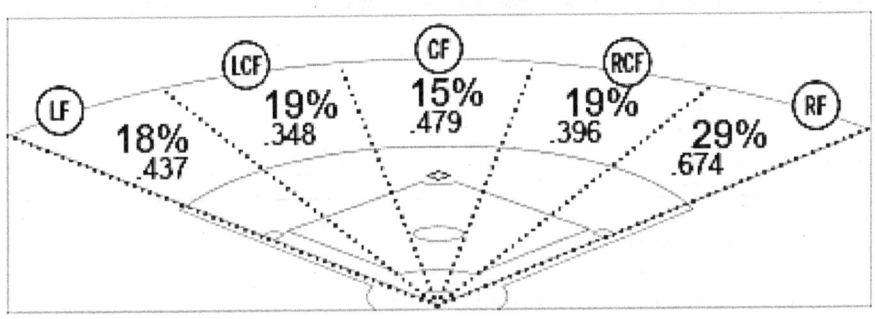

Strike Zone vs LHP   **Strike Zone vs RHP**

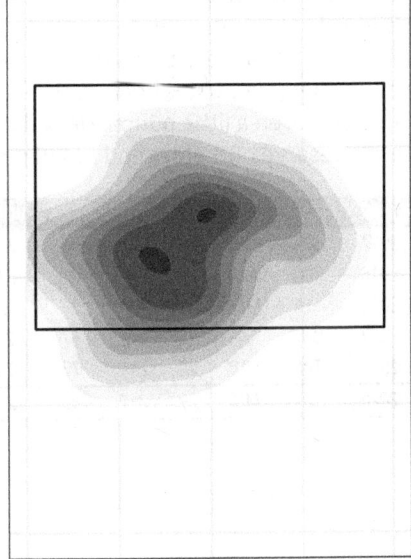

Guillermo Heredia CF

Born: 01/31/91 Age: 29 Bats: R Throws: L
Height: 5'10" Weight: 195 Origin: International Free Agent, 2016

YEAR	TEAM	LVL	AGE	PA	R	2B	3B	HR	RBI	BB	K	SB	CS	AVG/OBP/SLG
2017	SEA	MLB	26	426	43	16	0	6	24	27	64	1	5	.249/.315/.337
2018	TAC	AAA	27	38	4	1	0	0	2	4	3	2	1	.276/.421/.310
2018	SEA	MLB	27	337	29	14	1	5	19	32	52	2	4	.236/.318/.342
2019	DUR	AAA	28	30	3	1	0	1	4	1	10	0	1	.214/.267/.357
2019	TBA	MLB	28	231	31	13	0	5	20	18	60	2	2	.225/.306/.363
2020	TBA	MLB	29	251	24	12	1	5	25	20	58	2	1	.233/.313/.361

Comparables: Chris Magruder, Charles Gipson, Bob Watson

Heredia shifted coasts, moving from the Pacific Northwest to the west coast of Florida. Unfortunately, the change in team, division and time zone did not make him a better hitter. Heredia is a really good fourth outfielder. He has speed and can play all three outfield positions—an important skill when your center fielder injures himself on an annual basis. In an ideal world, Heredia would be on the short side of a platoon in center, but when your entire marketing plan revolves around ol' blue eyes, it would be a tough sell to have him miss a quarter of the games. Heredia's bat is only viable against lefties where he shows bat-to-ball skills and even a little punch. He will continue to have a role somewhere as a useful reserve outfielder and noted party starter in the dugout and clubhouse.

YEAR	TEAM	LVL	AGE	PA	DRC+	VORP	BABIP	BRR	FRAA	WARP
2017	SEA	MLB	26	426	88	2.0	.284	1.0	CF(63): 7.1, LF(62): 1.7	1.8
2018	TAC	AAA	27	38	111	5.0	.296	0.9	LF(6): 1.0, CF(5): -0.5	0.3
2018	SEA	MLB	27	337	89	7.8	.270	0.0	CF(89): -6.5, LF(32): 3.1	0.3
2019	DUR	AAA	28	30	67	-2.1	.294	0.0	CF(8): -0.2	0.0
2019	TBA	MLB	28	231	77	0.5	.293	2.0	CF(41): 0.5, RF(28): 0.8	0.4
2020	TBA	MLB	29	251	83	3.6	.291	1.1	CF 1, LF 1	0.6

Guillermo Heredia, continued

Batted Ball Distribution

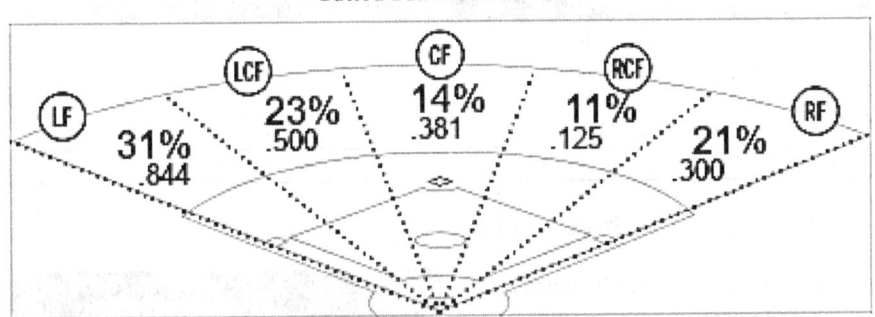

Strike Zone vs LHP   Strike Zone vs RHP

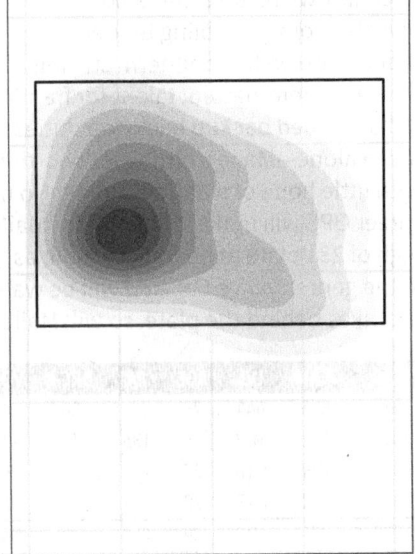

Luke Maile C

Born: 02/06/91 Age: 29 Bats: R Throws: R
Height: 6'3" Weight: 225 Origin: Round 8, 2012 Draft (#272 overall)

YEAR	TEAM	LVL	AGE	PA	R	2B	3B	HR	RBI	BB	K	SB	CS	AVG/OBP/SLG
2017	BUF	AAA	26	58	5	0	0	1	4	12	0	0	0	.167/.224/.167
2017	TOR	MLB	26	136	10	5	0	2	7	3	35	1	0	.146/.176/.231
2018	TOR	MLB	27	231	22	13	1	3	27	25	67	2	0	.248/.333/.366
2019	TOR	MLB	28	129	9	2	1	2	9	8	33	1	0	.151/.205/.235
2020	PIT	MLB	29	259	21	11	1	5	23	19	70	1	0	.190/.256/.299

Comparables: John Buck, Joel Skinner, Matt Wieters

Like many classic romantic comedies, *You've Got Mail* is formulaic and reflects, two decades after its release, some troubling gender attitudes. Luke Maile, well more than two decades after his own release, has also revealed some troubling tendencies that bog down his long-term staying

YEAR	TEAM	P. COUNT	FRM RUNS	BLK RUNS	THRW RUNS	TOT RUNS
2017	BUF	1555	3.3	0.2	0.0	3.2
2017	TOR	5503	3.8	0.8	0.2	3.9
2018	TOR	9089	8.1	0.1	0.1	8.2
2019	TOR	5996	5.2	0.8	0.3	6.3
2020	PIT	11629	6.6	0.0	0.4	7.0

power. A preternatural talent for framing, Maile (don't call him the Tom Hanks of it) has earned backup backstop duties almost on that ability alone. And I do mean alone—Maile's hitting is "two-thirds through a rom-com" grim, except with little hope of a happy ending. No matter the utility of frame jobs, a .556 career OPS will make it difficult for Maile to ever receive more than his career high of 231 plate appearances. Still, as long as it's available as a featured movie in the genre, *You've Got Mail* will be watched, and as long as he can steal bushels of strikes behind the plate, so will Maile.

YEAR	TEAM	LVL	AGE	PA	DRC+	VORP	BABIP	BRR	FRAA	WARP
2017	BUF	AAA	26	58	36	-4.8	.214	0.4	C(13): 3.3	0.2
2017	TOR	MLB	26	136	47	-7.1	.181	0.2	C(46): 4.3	0.2
2018	TOR	MLB	27	231	85	8.6	.351	0.2	C(66): 9.5	1.7
2019	TOR	MLB	28	129	55	-0.8	.190	-0.2	C(44): 7.2, P(2): 0.0	0.6
2020	PIT	MLB	29	259	47	-6.0	.248	-0.1	C 7	0.2

Luke Maile, continued

Batted Ball Distribution

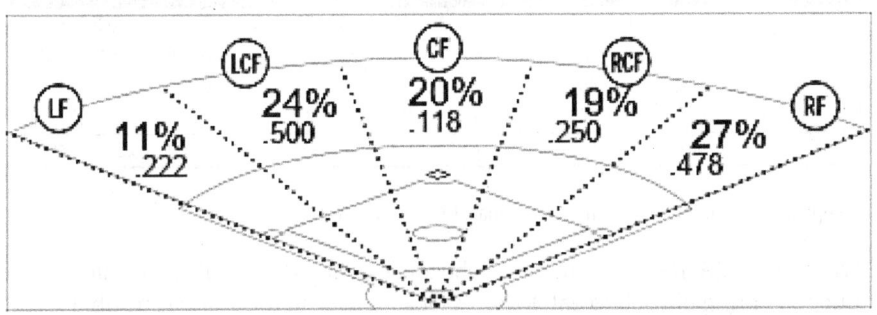

Strike Zone vs LHP   **Strike Zone vs RHP**

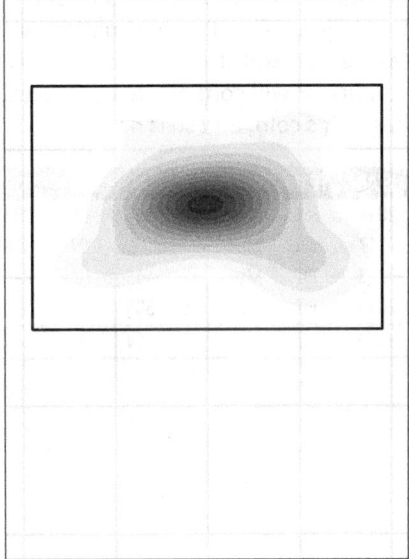

Pittsburgh Pirates 2020

Colin Moran 3B

Born: 10/01/92 Age: 27 Bats: L Throws: R
Height: 6'4" Weight: 205 Origin: Round 1, 2013 Draft (#6 overall)

YEAR	TEAM	LVL	AGE	PA	R	2B	3B	HR	RBI	BB	K	SB	CS	AVG/OBP/SLG
2017	FRE	AAA	24	338	53	15	1	18	63	31	55	0	3	.308/.373/.543
2017	HOU	MLB	24	12	3	0	1	1	3	1	1	0	0	.364/.417/.818
2018	PIT	MLB	25	465	49	19	1	11	58	39	82	0	2	.277/.340/.407
2019	PIT	MLB	26	503	46	30	1	13	80	30	117	0	1	.277/.322/.429
2020	PIT	MLB	27	504	53	27	1	14	58	37	115	1	1	.259/.318/.415

Comparables: Brandon Drury, Lonnie Chisenhall, Cheslor Cuthbert

WESTCHESTER, NY—Local man eyes bacon, egg and cheese on everything bagel, but can't bring himself to eat. Moran's lack of place in the world is troubling him. Sure, he's been successful all things considered. But he's seemingly plateaued, and a younger, more promising coworker is on the cusp of usurping him. Maybe he's just another millennial plagued with existential angst, tormented with thoughts of living up to his surname. After all, Moran's uncle played 19 years in the majors—and, to make matters worse, his brother debuted with the Marlins last season and struck him out for his first career punch out. He is fearful that conditions will continue to deteriorate. That's life, he reasons. He bites into the bagel. It's cold, and so is he.

YEAR	TEAM	LVL	AGE	PA	DRC+	VORP	BABIP	BRR	FRAA	WARP
2017	FRE	AAA	24	338	134	28.9	.323	-0.3	3B(57): 0.3, 1B(15): -1.7	2.3
2017	HOU	MLB	24	12	97	2.5	.333	0.6	1B(4): -0.1, 3B(3): -0.2	0.0
2018	PIT	MLB	25	465	100	22.7	.316	-1.5	3B(116): -2.7	1.2
2019	PIT	MLB	26	503	84	8.1	.341	-0.7	3B(121): -18.7, 2B(11): 0.1	-1.1
2020	PIT	MLB	27	504	93	7.9	.315	-0.2	3B -7	0.1

Colin Moran, *continued*

Batted Ball Distribution

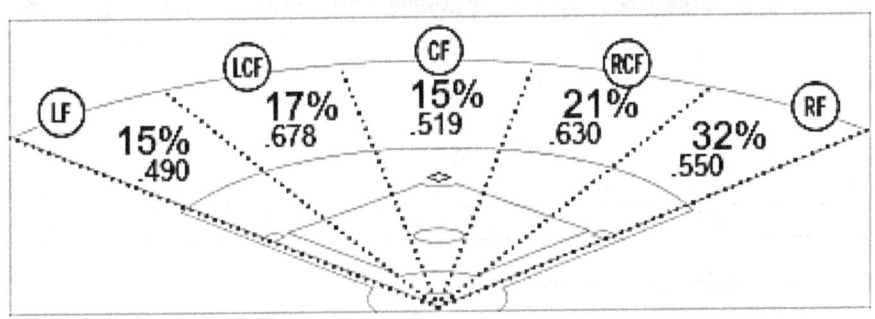

Strike Zone vs LHP   **Strike Zone vs RHP**

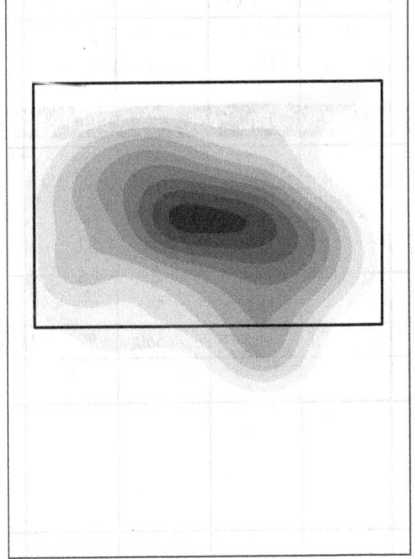

Kevin Newman SS

Born: 08/04/93 Age: 26 Bats: R Throws: R
Height: 6'0" Weight: 195 Origin: Round 1, 2015 Draft (#19 overall)

YEAR	TEAM	LVL	AGE	PA	R	2B	3B	HR	RBI	BB	K	SB	CS	AVG/OBP/SLG
2017	ALT	AA	23	375	42	18	2	4	30	22	40	4	2	.259/.310/.359
2017	IND	AAA	23	178	23	11	2	0	11	7	22	7	1	.283/.314/.373
2018	IND	AAA	24	477	74	30	2	4	35	31	50	28	11	.302/.350/.407
2018	PIT	MLB	24	97	7	2	0	0	6	4	23	0	1	.209/.247/.231
2019	IND	AAA	25	35	5	2	0	0	1	5	7	0	1	.233/.343/.300
2019	PIT	MLB	25	531	61	20	6	12	64	28	62	16	8	.308/.353/.446
2020	PIT	MLB	26	560	53	27	3	9	55	33	75	11	4	.270/.320/.385

Comparables: Angel Berroa, Ramón Torres, Tony Kemp

A former first-round pick from Arizona acquitted himself well in the bigs, Newman showcased his plus (or thereabout) hit tool often enough to make up for the concerns about his glove. He has a limited profile at the plate since he doesn't walk much and entered the season with 15 home runs for his career. In other words, Newman will have to keep his average up to have value, so his path forward is a little more complicated than his rookie-year production indicates.

YEAR	TEAM	LVL	AGE	PA	DRC+	VORP	BABIP	BRR	FRAA	WARP
2017	ALT	AA	23	375	92	14.6	.282	1.4	SS(81): 0.6	1.6
2017	IND	AAA	23	178	85	4.9	.324	-1.3	SS(38): 0.4	0.4
2018	IND	AAA	24	477	126	32.8	.333	3.2	SS(83): 2.9, 2B(21): -0.6	3.7
2018	PIT	MLB	24	97	62	-4.1	.275	-0.6	SS(24): -1.4, 2B(8): -0.7	-0.3
2019	IND	AAA	25	35	85	0.1	.304	0.7	SS(4): -0.4, LF(2): -0.3	0.1
2019	PIT	MLB	25	531	107	28.9	.333	0.9	SS(104): -1.3, 2B(23): 0.0	2.8
2020	PIT	MLB	26	560	89	13.5	.302	0.7	SS -1, 2B 0	1.3

Kevin Newman, continued

Batted Ball Distribution

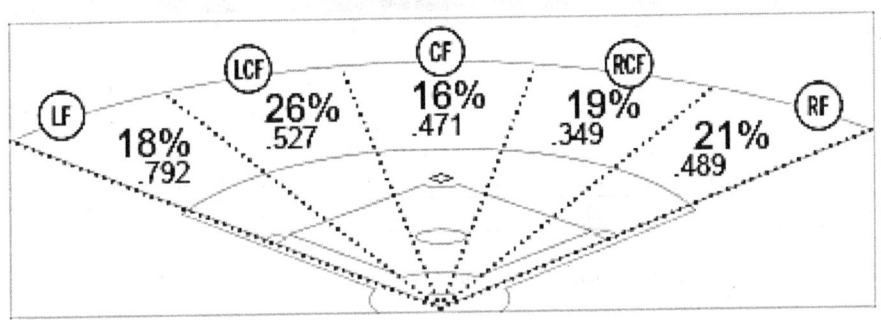

Strike Zone vs LHP   **Strike Zone vs RHP**

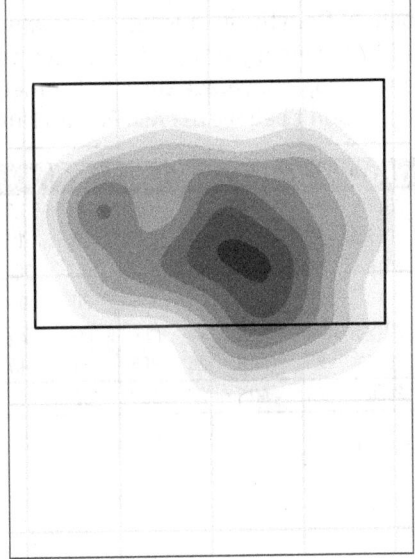

Pittsburgh Pirates 2020

José Osuna 4C

Born: 12/12/92 Age: 27 Bats: R Throws: R
Height: 6'2" Weight: 240 Origin: International Free Agent, 2009

YEAR	TEAM	LVL	AGE	PA	R	2B	3B	HR	RBI	BB	K	SB	CS	AVG/OBP/SLG
2017	IND	AAA	24	41	6	5	0	0	1	5	9	1	1	.250/.341/.389
2017	PIT	MLB	24	227	31	13	4	7	30	9	40	0	0	.233/.269/.428
2018	IND	AAA	25	342	45	26	0	9	59	31	51	5	3	.321/.378/.497
2018	PIT	MLB	25	111	14	9	0	3	11	3	22	0	0	.226/.252/.396
2019	IND	AAA	26	83	13	7	1	2	13	9	22	2	0	.268/.361/.479
2019	PIT	MLB	26	285	41	20	0	10	36	18	48	0	0	.264/.310/.456
2020	PIT	MLB	27	308	31	19	1	10	37	19	61	2	1	.236/.289/.412

Comparables: C.J. Cron, Brett Wallace, Yonder Alonso

If we had to, we'd guess that Osuna is a proponent of the universal DH. The lack of a defensive home meant he received fewer plate appearances last season than various, less potent Pirates, like Elias Díaz (he can catch), Colin Moran (he can stand at third) and Melky Cabrera (web design is his passion). Osuna would benefit from the AL ruleset, under which all he would need to concern himself with is swinging through four or five plate appearances a game. He might be only a league-average stick, but sometimes that's enough to receive serious burn. Don't believe us? Ask Renato Nuñez.

YEAR	TEAM	LVL	AGE	PA	DRC+	VORP	BABIP	BRR	FRAA	WARP
2017	IND	AAA	24	41	114	1.3	.333	0.1	1B(6): -0.2, RF(2): 0.0	0.1
2017	PIT	MLB	24	227	78	-1.5	.254	-0.7	RF(25): -0.4, 1B(23): -1.1	-0.3
2018	IND	AAA	25	342	163	30.5	.353	1.4	3B(47): 4.6, 1B(24): -0.7	3.8
2018	PIT	MLB	25	111	80	0.7	.256	0.8	1B(12): 1.9, 3B(7): -0.2	0.3
2019	IND	AAA	26	83	114	2.7	.354	0.2	RF(12): -2.6, LF(3): -0.2	0.1
2019	PIT	MLB	26	285	94	4.7	.285	-1.1	1B(31): 1.2, RF(23): -0.5	0.6
2020	PIT	MLB	27	308	82	-0.3	.267	-0.4	3B 1, RF 0	0.1

José Osuna, continued

Batted Ball Distribution

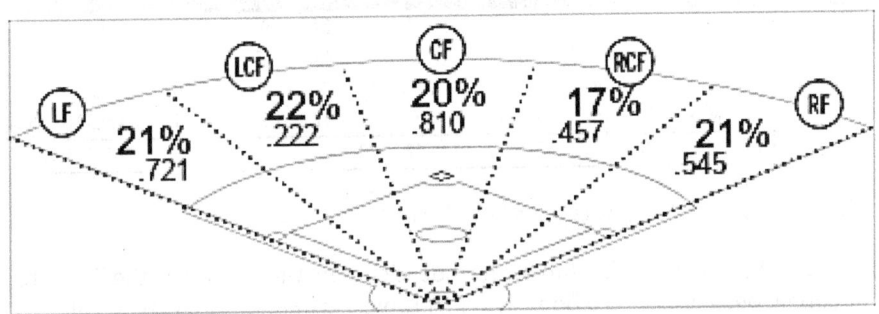

Strike Zone vs LHP

Strike Zone vs RHP

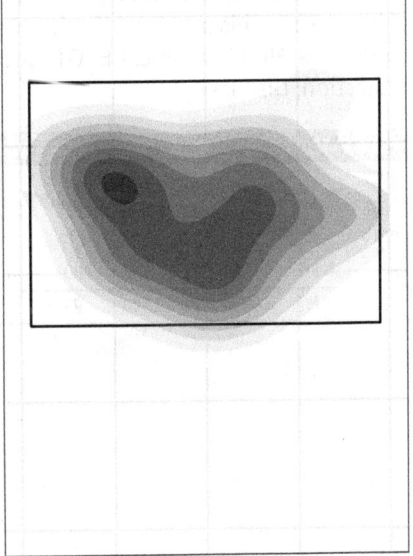

Pittsburgh Pirates 2020

Gregory Polanco RF

Born: 09/14/91   Age: 28   Bats: L   Throws: L
Height: 6'5"   Weight: 235   Origin: International Free Agent, 2009

YEAR	TEAM	LVL	AGE	PA	R	2B	3B	HR	RBI	BB	K	SB	CS	AVG/OBP/SLG
2017	PIT	MLB	25	411	39	20	0	11	35	27	60	8	1	.251/.305/.391
2018	PIT	MLB	26	535	75	32	6	23	81	61	117	12	2	.254/.340/.499
2019	IND	AAA	27	54	5	4	0	1	11	9	16	2	0	.267/.389/.422
2019	PIT	MLB	27	167	23	8	1	6	17	12	49	3	1	.242/.301/.425
2020	PIT	MLB	28	574	63	33	3	19	70	54	147	15	5	.241/.315/.425

Comparables: Jake Marisnick, Marcell Ozuna, Dave Winfield

Welcome back to El Coffee Talk with Linda Richman. Unfortunately the lines are not open, because this is a book. Our first topic, his injured shoulder. We all know it underwent surgery two autumns ago, but aggravating it a couple times, the poor kid, curbed all but a month of his 2019. That's his throwing arm, which used to be like buttah, but now it's just like matzah. The second topic, his rare combination of speed and power should return, but for how long? The thought of him passing his prime can make one a little verklempt. Talk amongst yourselves. Here's a topic. PECOTA projections are neither PECOTA nor a projection: Discuss.

YEAR	TEAM	LVL	AGE	PA	DRC+	VORP	BABIP	BRR	FRAA	WARP
2017	PIT	MLB	25	411	87	2.8	.272	0.5	RF(68): 4.1, LF(25): -2.6	0.5
2018	PIT	MLB	26	535	107	29.7	.287	0.7	RF(124): 1.3	1.8
2019	IND	AAA	27	54	112	3.5	.393	1.0	RF(8): -1.1	0.2
2019	PIT	MLB	27	167	80	-0.4	.316	0.5	RF(36): 0.4	0.0
2020	PIT	MLB	28	574	93	8.9	.300	-0.1	RF 1, SS 0	1.0

Gregory Polanco, continued

Batted Ball Distribution

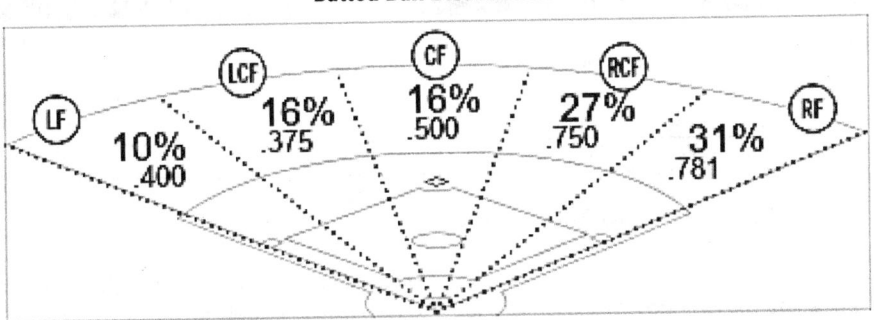

Strike Zone vs LHP **Strike Zone vs RHP**

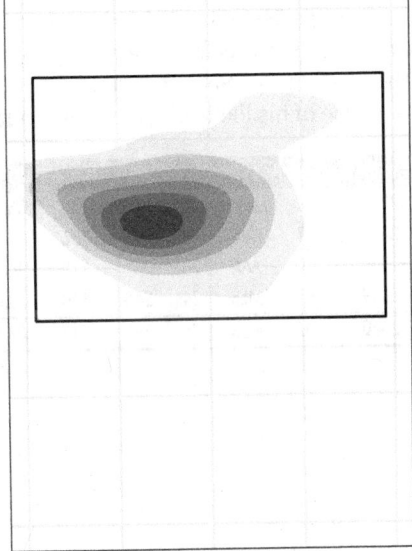

Bryan Reynolds LF

Born: 01/27/95   Age: 25   Bats: B   Throws: R
Height: 6'3"   Weight: 205   Origin: Round 2, 2016 Draft (#59 overall)

YEAR	TEAM	LVL	AGE	PA	R	2B	3B	HR	RBI	BB	K	SB	CS	AVG/OBP/SLG
2017	SJO	A+	22	541	72	26	9	10	63	37	106	5	3	.312/.364/.462
2018	ALT	AA	23	383	56	18	3	7	46	43	73	4	4	.302/.381/.438
2019	IND	AAA	24	57	10	1	1	5	11	7	11	3	2	.367/.446/.735
2019	PIT	MLB	24	546	83	37	4	16	68	46	121	3	2	.314/.377/.503
2020	PIT	MLB	25	595	67	35	4	17	73	49	138	2	1	.283/.349/.458

Comparables: Joe Adcock, Lance Berkman, Zoilo Almonte

Rookie of the Year predictions border on pseudoscience. The top challenge is guessing playing time, with deference given to players likely to make the team out of camp. Reynolds, the positional counterpart in the Andrew McCutchen deal, was one of those Swiss army knife outfielders (does a little bit of everything, and also your dad keeps telling you that you need one wherever you go) who rightfully began in Triple-A, yet injuries led to plenty of Pittsburgh-based reps. He not only held his own but nearly captured the league batting title and demonstrated a competent power game. We'd suggest he should be one of the favorites for Second Year Player of the Year—because of his play and because of his likely playing time—but that would be sophomoric.

YEAR	TEAM	LVL	AGE	PA	DRC+	VORP	BABIP	BRR	FRAA	WARP
2017	SJO	A+	22	541	140	35.6	.376	-0.9	CF(50): -4.3, RF(42): -2.9	2.7
2018	ALT	AA	23	383	136	33.4	.362	-0.2	CF(43): -3.2, LF(42): -3.6	2.0
2019	IND	AAA	24	57	178	9.8	.394	-0.7	CF(13): -1.3	0.5
2019	PIT	MLB	24	546	110	23.0	.387	1.5	LF(79): -0.4, RF(31): 0.1	2.2
2020	PIT	MLB	25	595	113	27.5	.352	1.3	LF -2, RF 0	2.6

Bryan Reynolds, continued

Batted Ball Distribution

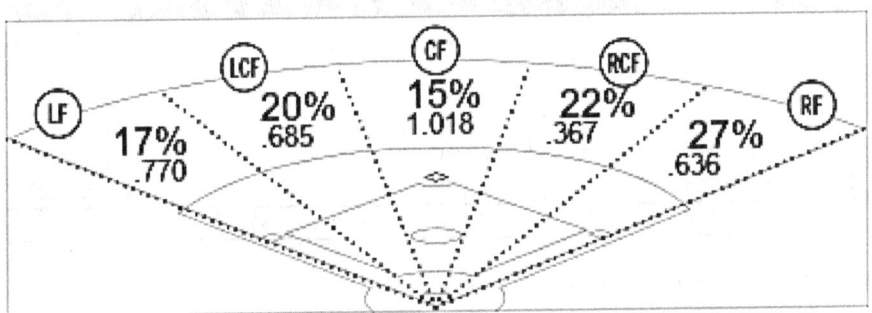

Strike Zone vs LHP   **Strike Zone vs RHP**

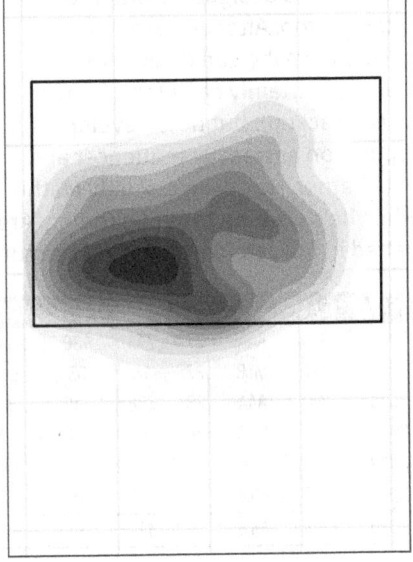

Jacob Stallings C

Born: 12/22/89 Age: 30 Bats: R Throws: R
Height: 6'4" Weight: 220 Origin: Round 7, 2012 Draft (#226 overall)

YEAR	TEAM	LVL	AGE	PA	R	2B	3B	HR	RBI	BB	K	SB	CS	AVG/OBP/SLG
2017	IND	AAA	27	243	35	16	0	4	38	17	30	1	2	.301/.358/.431
2017	PIT	MLB	27	16	3	2	0	0	3	2	2	0	0	.357/.438/.500
2018	IND	AAA	28	278	37	22	1	3	40	15	51	1	2	.285/.335/.414
2018	PIT	MLB	28	41	2	0	0	0	5	3	9	0	0	.216/.268/.216
2019	IND	AAA	29	61	11	9	0	2	7	4	9	0	0	.275/.361/.569
2019	PIT	MLB	29	210	26	5	0	6	13	16	40	0	0	.262/.325/.382
2020	PIT	MLB	30	427	40	21	1	10	44	25	93	2	1	.235/.290/.365

Comparables: Bryan Holaday, Brett Nicholas, Chad Moeller

We're just about there with pitchers, and so 25 years from now it's entirely possible we throw up our arms and implement a designated hitter for catchers, too. After all, rare is the pitch-caller who can do everything. Stallings certainly can't (and for that he is a backup), but he is developing a reputation as a savvy sequencer and

YEAR	TEAM	P. COUNT	FRM RUNS	BLK RUNS	THRW RUNS	TOT RUNS
2017	IND	8388	-4.6	-0.3	0.4	-5.2
2017	PIT	634	-0.2	0.2	0.0	-1.1
2018	IND	8927	-6.1	0.3	-0.1	-5.3
2018	PIT	1468	-0.7	0.5	0.0	0.9
2019	IND	2141	0.9	0.0	0.1	1.4
2019	PIT	7704	8.7	3.6	0.3	13.0
2020	PIT	16361	1.3	3.9	1.2	6.4

elite framer. He doesn't exactly Mathis it at the plate but all of his value comes when he's wearing tons of padding. Are we saying he'd be an All-Star hitter if he batted in full catching gear? It'd be stupid not to try.

YEAR	TEAM	LVL	AGE	PA	DRC+	VORP	BABIP	BRR	FRAA	WARP
2017	IND	AAA	27	243	130	20.4	.330	1.2	C(60): -4.3, 1B(1): -0.1	1.5
2017	PIT	MLB	27	16	83	3.0	.417	0.5	C(5): -0.1	0.1
2018	IND	AAA	28	278	119	15.4	.343	-1.4	C(63): -4.7	1.2
2018	PIT	MLB	28	41	74	-0.1	.276	0.5	C(13): 0.1	0.1
2019	IND	AAA	29	61	116	2.4	.286	-3.2	C(15): 0.6	0.2
2019	PIT	MLB	29	210	96	9.8	.303	0.6	C(61): 13.6, P(1): 0.0	2.3
2020	PIT	MLB	30	427	74	6.7	.284	1.2	C 8	1.5

Jacob Stallings, continued

Batted Ball Distribution

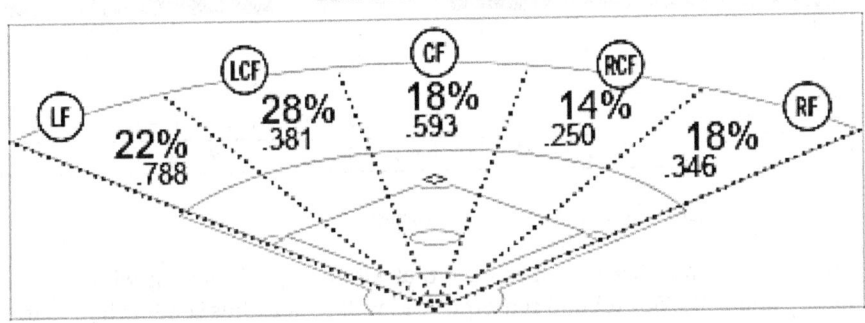

| Strike Zone vs LHP | Strike Zone vs RHP |

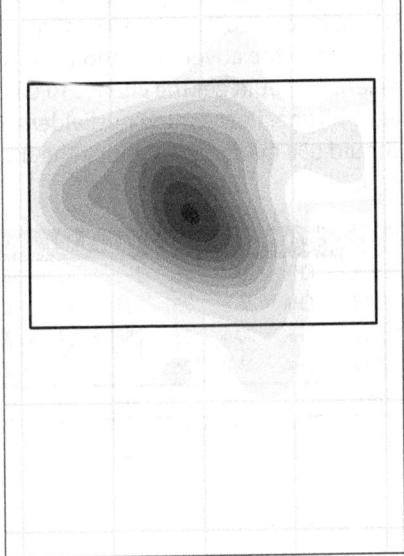

Charles Tilson OF

Born: 12/02/92   Age: 27   Bats: L   Throws: L
Height: 6'0"   Weight: 185   Origin: Round 2, 2011 Draft (#79 overall)

YEAR	TEAM	LVL	AGE	PA	R	2B	3B	HR	RBI	BB	K	SB	CS	AVG/OBP/SLG
2018	CHR	AAA	25	292	27	12	0	0	25	16	52	10	2	.244/.288/.289
2018	CHA	MLB	25	121	7	1	1	0	11	10	20	2	3	.264/.331/.292
2019	CHR	AAA	26	258	36	13	2	3	34	19	43	4	3	.288/.345/.398
2019	CHA	MLB	26	157	16	5	0	1	12	10	38	4	0	.229/.293/.285
2020	CHA	MLB	27	251	21	10	1	3	21	16	54	9	3	.238/.293/.324

Comparables: Ezequiel Carrera, Rey Fuentes, Dalton Pompey

Surely more than a few people noticed that within days of colliding with left fielder and White Sox rebuild centerpiece Eloy Jiménez (thus sending him to the injured list), Tilson was on a plane back to Charlotte, where he spent the final six weeks of the minor-league season. Of course, eight hits over his last month-plus in Chicago was also possibly a culprit in his demise. Tilson was never supposed to make a living hitting for power, but save for a wacky moment in Houston where he turned around a 98-mph Josh James fastball for a grand slam, he's lived up to the advertising too well. Tilson will enter 2020 out of options, which means he could get the chance to climb his way up another club's totem pole of light-hitting, fleet-footed outfielders. If given the opportunity, next time he should use his speed to dodge the franchise cornerstone—you know, just in case.

YEAR	TEAM	LVL	AGE	PA	DRC+	VORP	BABIP	BRR	FRAA	WARP
2018	CHR	AAA	25	292	67	-5.1	.301	1.4	CF(49): -3.1, LF(17): -0.7	-0.3
2018	CHA	MLB	25	121	72	-0.7	.322	0.7	LF(32): -0.3, CF(5): -0.2	-0.1
2019	CHR	AAA	26	258	87	2.3	.340	1.5	LF(35): 1.0, CF(23): -3.7	0.2
2019	CHA	MLB	26	157	68	-2.3	.305	2.3	RF(30): 2.7, LF(19): -0.9	0.3
2020	CHA	MLB	27	251	65	-1.9	.300	1.3	CF 1, LF 0	-0.1

Charles Tilson, continued

Batted Ball Distribution

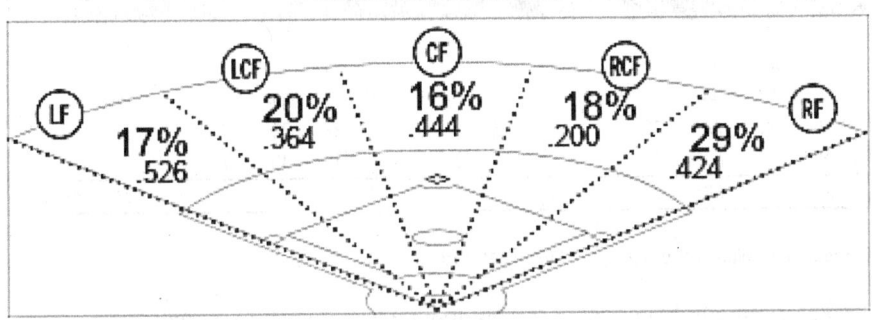

Strike Zone vs LHP **Strike Zone vs RHP**

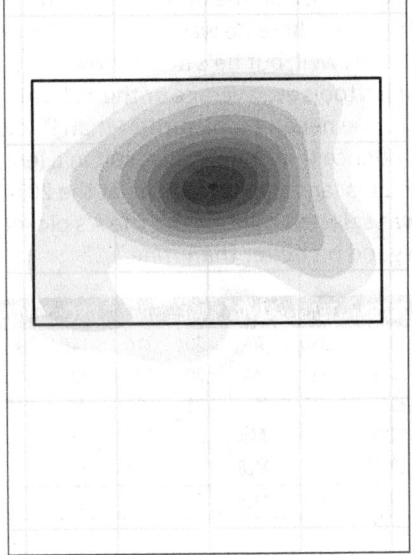

Cole Tucker SS

Born: 07/03/96 Age: 23 Bats: B Throws: R
Height: 6'3" Weight: 205 Origin: Round 1, 2014 Draft (#24 overall)

YEAR	TEAM	LVL	AGE	PA	R	2B	3B	HR	RBI	BB	K	SB	CS	AVG/OBP/SLG
2017	BRD	A+	20	316	46	15	6	4	32	34	70	36	12	.285/.364/.426
2017	ALT	AA	20	194	25	4	5	2	18	21	31	11	3	.257/.349/.377
2018	ALT	AA	21	589	77	21	7	5	44	55	104	35	12	.259/.333/.356
2019	IND	AAA	22	353	51	15	4	8	28	38	73	11	3	.261/.346/.413
2019	PIT	MLB	22	159	16	10	3	2	13	10	40	0	0	.211/.266/.361
2020	PIT	MLB	23	189	17	8	2	3	17	14	47	6	3	.216/.280/.337

Comparables: Willi Castro, Jonathan Villar, Tyler Wade

Tucker's immediate impact at the big-league level may have convinced some that he was fit to be Pittsburgh's shortstop by the combination of his play (he recorded three hits, all for extra bases, in his first three games); his dynamic flow; and general bushy tailed optimism. Alas, the former first-round pick failed to capitalize on the opportunity, and instead spent most of the 2019 season in Triple-A, where he was fine. "Fine" is about the upshot here. Tucker runs and throws well, but he's never grown into power despite a 6-foot-3 frame. The rest of his tools are average or thereabout. There's still a big-league future here; after all, one needn't look further than Pittsburgh's recent history of shortstops for evidence that "fine" can result in a lengthy career. Even so, we would advise Pirates fans against looking at the 2014 draft—lest they remember that Tucker was selected right before the A's picked Matt Chapman, who, we can all agree, is a good bit better than "fine."

YEAR	TEAM	LVL	AGE	PA	DRC+	VORP	BABIP	BRR	FRAA	WARP
2017	BRD	A+	20	316	146	30.5	.368	1.5	SS(66): -0.4	2.7
2017	ALT	AA	20	194	100	11.6	.304	1.3	SS(42): 0.9	1.1
2018	ALT	AA	21	589	92	37.5	.310	3.4	SS(131): -0.6	2.4
2019	IND	AAA	22	353	102	15.2	.319	1.2	SS(69): -4.7, 2B(6): 0.8	1.3
2019	PIT	MLB	22	159	62	-0.3	.276	1.3	SS(45): -1.1	0.0
2020	PIT	MLB	23	189	65	-0.9	.278	0.5	SS 0, 2B 0	-0.1

Cole Tucker, continued

Batted Ball Distribution

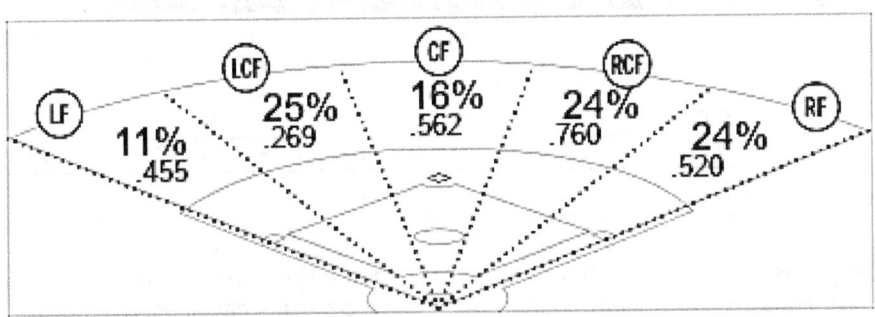

Strike Zone vs LHP   **Strike Zone vs RHP**

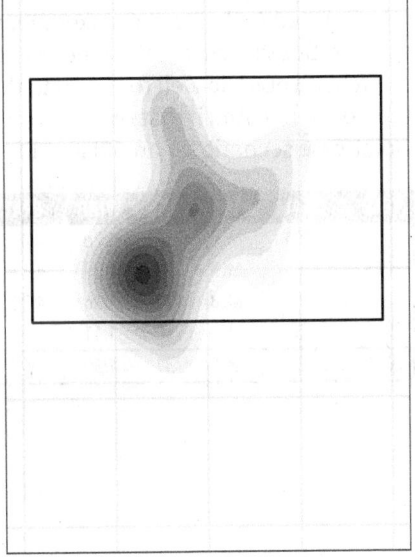

Chris Archer RHP

Born: 09/26/88 Age: 31 Bats: R Throws: R
Height: 6'2" Weight: 195 Origin: Round 5, 2006 Draft (#161 overall)

YEAR	TEAM	LVL	AGE	W	L	SV	G	GS	IP	H	HR	BB/9	K/9	K	GB%	BABIP
2017	TBA	MLB	28	10	12	0	34	34	201	193	27	2.7	11.1	249	43%	.325
2018	TBA	MLB	29	3	5	0	17	17	96	102	11	2.9	9.6	102	46%	.343
2018	PIT	MLB	29	3	3	0	10	10	52^1	53	8	3.1	10.3	60	48%	.328
2019	PIT	MLB	30	3	9	0	23	23	119^2	114	25	4.1	10.8	143	38%	.298
2020	PIT	MLB	31	8	9	0	26	26	137	124	21	3.6	10.4	159	40%	.296

Comparables: Danny Salazar, Max Scherzer, Sonny Gray

Archer is suffering through the worst-case scenario Max Scherzer simulation. Five years ago, both seemed cut from the same cloth: fastball-slider dynamos who would rack up strikeouts if not complete games. Scherzer, of course, is a generational ace. Archer, conversely, wondering how both his ERA and FIP have crept above five. The easy answer is: the Pirates. The longer answer is...no, it's almost certainly the Pirates. Ex-pitching coach Ray Searage notoriously reintroduced Archer to the sinkerball, a tool he abandoned after 2014 to much success. But those were the types of decisions that cost Searage his job last year, so Archer would do well to return to the three-pitch mix that once made him a top-10 pitcher. And if that doesn't work, he may have to experience the extreme worst-case scenario for an old ace: life as a late-inning reliever.

YEAR	TEAM	LVL	AGE	WHIP	ERA	DRA	WARP	MPH	FB%	WHF	CSP
2017	TBA	MLB	28	1.26	4.07	3.53	4.6	97.8	47.4	14.6	47.4
2018	TBA	MLB	29	1.39	4.31	4.12	1.3	97.2	45.6	14.3	48.6
2018	PIT	MLB	29	1.36	4.30	4.30	0.6	96.9	49.3	13.2	45.6
2019	PIT	MLB	30	1.41	5.19	4.42	1.8	96.1	50.5	13.5	45.2
2020	PIT	MLB	31	1.30	4.07	4.23	2.4	96.1	48	13.9	46.3

Chris Archer, continued

Pitch Shape vs LHH

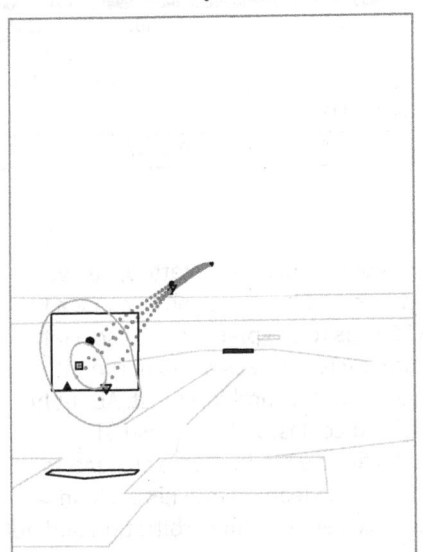

Pitch Shape vs RHH

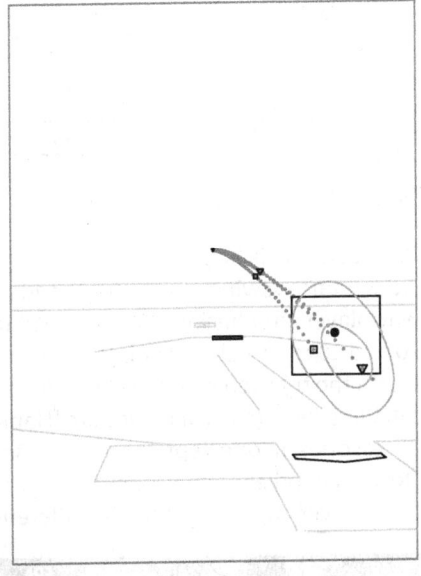

Type	Frequency	Velocity	H Movement	V Movement
● Fastball	43.2%	94.2 [105]	-6.1 [103]	-11.8 [111]
◻ Sinker	7.3%	94.5 [110]	-9.8 [118]	-13.5 [124]
✛ Cutter				
▲ Changeup	12.0%	87.9 [110]	-10.4 [103]	-24.3 [109]
✕ Splitter				
▽ Slider	35.5%	88.9 [119]	5 [100]	-28.9 [112]
◇ Curveball				
⬥ Slow Curveball				
✳ Knuckleball				
▼ Screwball				

Steven Brault LHP

Born: 04/29/92 Age: 28 Bats: L Throws: L
Height: 6'0" Weight: 195 Origin: Round 11, 2013 Draft (#339 overall)

YEAR	TEAM	LVL	AGE	W	L	SV	G	GS	IP	H	HR	BB/9	K/9	K	GB%	BABIP
2017	IND	AAA	25	10	5	0	21	20	120^1	85	5	3.3	8.2	109	53%	.252
2017	PIT	MLB	25	1	0	1	11	4	34^2	41	3	3.6	6.0	23	45%	.317
2018	PIT	MLB	26	6	3	0	45	5	91^2	84	10	5.6	8.1	82	50%	.289
2019	PIT	MLB	27	4	6	0	25	19	113^1	117	15	4.2	7.9	100	45%	.310
2020	PIT	MLB	28	7	9	0	26	26	132	133	18	4.2	8.0	117	45%	.299

Comparables: Michael Kirkman, Adam Conley, André Rienzo

Brault wears his hobbies on his sleeve, or as part of his sleeve tattoo, anyway. He's a starter/swingman, a singer and a gamer, and he may soon become a two-way player after hitting .333/.349/.429 in 50 trips to the plate. (He's also a lefty, so add 10 more eclectic points.) Brault's athleticism makes the experiment worth the try even if he's likely to remain a hurler first and foremost. About his pitching: his pitches of choice are [Hank Hill voice] fastballs and fastball accessories. In one September start, Brault's first 69 pitches were all heaters. He's not good enough to stick in a rotation, and so leaning into his protean nature even more might be the difference between reaching arbitration and not.

YEAR	TEAM	LVL	AGE	WHIP	ERA	DRA	WARP	MPH	FB%	WHF	CSP
2017	IND	AAA	25	1.07	1.94	2.85	3.8				
2017	PIT	MLB	25	1.59	4.67	6.17	-0.3	93.9	72	8.8	46.8
2018	PIT	MLB	26	1.54	4.61	5.66	-0.7	95.2	65	10.8	46.9
2019	PIT	MLB	27	1.50	5.16	4.40	1.6	94.1	64.3	10.5	47
2020	PIT	MLB	28	1.47	4.88	4.86	1.4	93.9	65.7	10.5	47.2

Steven Brault, continued

Pitch Shape vs LHH

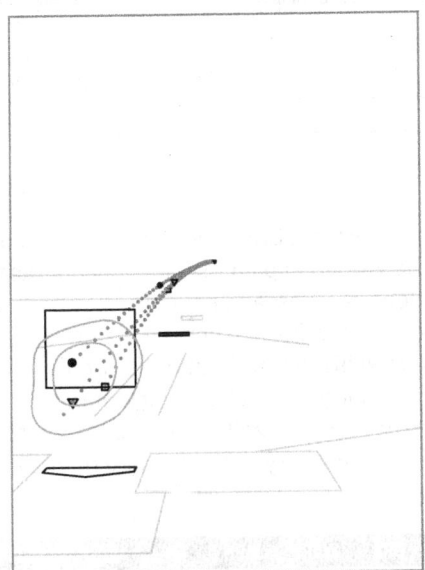

Pitch Shape vs RHH

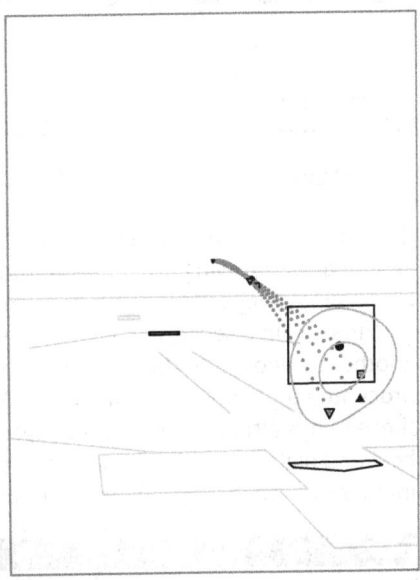

Type	Frequency	Velocity	H Movement	V Movement
● Fastball	48.7%	92.5 [100]	8.5 [92]	-17.1 [97]
□ Sinker	15.6%	91.6 [95]	12.8 [99]	-23.6 [89]
+ Cutter				
▲ Changeup	13.9%	84.7 [98]	9.6 [107]	-32.3 [86]
✕ Splitter				
▽ Slider	21.0%	83.1 [95]	-5.1 [100]	-36.4 [90]
◇ Curveball				
◈ Slow Curveball				
✳ Knuckleball				
▼ Screwball				

Nick Burdi RHP

Born: 01/19/93 Age: 27 Bats: R Throws: R
Height: 6'3" Weight: 225 Origin: Round 2, 2014 Draft (#46 overall)

YEAR	TEAM	LVL	AGE	W	L	SV	G	GS	IP	H	HR	BB/9	K/9	K	GB%	BABIP
2017	CHT	AA	24	2	0	1	14	0	17	9	1	2.1	10.6	20	46%	.222
2018	PIT	MLB	25	0	0	0	2	0	1^1	3	1	13.5	13.5	2	33%	.400
2019	PIT	MLB	26	2	1	0	11	0	8^2	11	1	3.1	17.7	17	20%	.526
2020	PIT	MLB	27	2	2	0	34	0	36	31	6	3.7	13.7	55	36%	.326

Comparables: Akeel Morris, Harvey Garcia, Mauricio Cabrera

It was a 1-0 pitch to Jarrod Dyson, a 97-mph fastball. Burdi released it, and then clutched his throwing arm and knelt to the ground in pain. He had been marked by a scalpel two winters ago for Tommy John reasons, and now this. Fortunately, in a sense, it wasn't the tendon but rather the nerve. He saw another surgeon, and this time they corrected his thoracic outlet syndrome (a procedure that should be called Chris Young surgery if we're going to name these things after players). Burdi ought to be ready to reaffirm his reputation for heat and high-leverage tolerance come spring. He'll try to throw more than 20 innings in a season for the first time since 2015.

YEAR	TEAM	LVL	AGE	WHIP	ERA	DRA	WARP	MPH	FB%	WHF	CSP
2017	CHT	AA	24	0.76	0.53	2.61	0.4				
2018	PIT	MLB	25	3.75	20.25	1.82	0.0	99.0	71.4	14.3	46.9
2019	PIT	MLB	26	1.62	9.35	2.67	0.3	98.6	45.3	18.9	49.5
2020	PIT	MLB	27	1.28	4.02	4.17	0.5	98.2	49.8	18.4	48.9

Nick Burdi, continued

Pitch Shape vs LHH

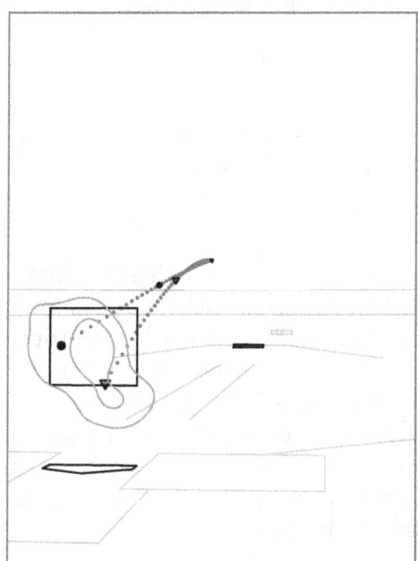

Pitch Shape vs RHH

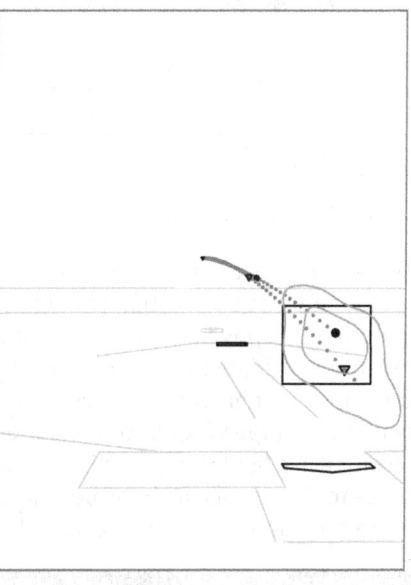

Type	Frequency	Velocity	H Movement	V Movement
● Fastball	45.3%	97.3 [114]	-5.8 [104]	-11.3 [112]
☐ Sinker				
+ Cutter				
▲ Changeup				
✕ Splitter				
▽ Slider	54.7%	88.2 [116]	3.2 [92]	-29.7 [110]
◇ Curveball				
⊕ Slow Curveball				
✱ Knuckleball				
▼ Screwball				

Pittsburgh Pirates 2020

Kyle Crick RHP
Born: 11/30/92   Age: 27   Bats: L   Throws: R
Height: 6'4"   Weight: 220   Origin: Round 1, 2011 Draft (#49 overall)

YEAR	TEAM	LVL	AGE	W	L	SV	G	GS	IP	H	HR	BB/9	K/9	K	GB%	BABIP
2017	SAC	AAA	24	1	2	6	24	0	29^1	24	1	4.0	12.0	39	45%	.329
2017	SFN	MLB	24	0	0	0	30	0	32^1	22	2	4.7	7.8	28	39%	.233
2018	PIT	MLB	25	3	2	2	64	0	60^1	45	3	3.4	9.7	65	43%	.268
2019	PIT	MLB	26	3	7	0	52	0	49	41	10	6.4	11.2	61	44%	.274
2020	PIT	MLB	27	3	3	5	57	0	60	51	8	4.7	10.4	69	42%	.286

Comparables: Trevor May, Sam Tuivailala, Neftalí Feliz

Athletes always want to make a name for themselves and win ballgames, and sometimes that entails maintaining a high intensity level. Crick made a name for himself by playing a small role in that wild Pirates-Reds fight, in which he tried to further infuriate Yasiel Puig (who, it must be noted, had technically been traded to another team minutes earlier). Later in the season, Crick infuriated teammate Felipe Vásquez over clubhouse music, according to various reports, resulting in a fight that precipitated a season-ending injury. We're nearly out of space to discuss his pitching, but that's what happens when a Personality gets into altercations. His pitching was adequate, by the way.

YEAR	TEAM	LVL	AGE	WHIP	ERA	DRA	WARP	MPH	FB%	WHF	CSP
2017	SAC	AAA	24	1.26	2.76	2.41	0.9				
2017	SFN	MLB	24	1.21	3.06	4.29	0.3	97.2	74.5	12.1	45.7
2018	PIT	MLB	25	1.13	2.39	4.41	0.4	97.8	72.9	12.6	47.9
2019	PIT	MLB	26	1.55	4.96	5.56	-0.1	96.7	62.3	13.3	46.4
2020	PIT	MLB	27	1.37	4.23	4.26	0.8	96.8	69.3	13	47.3

Kyle Crick, continued

Pitch Shape vs LHH	Pitch Shape vs RHH
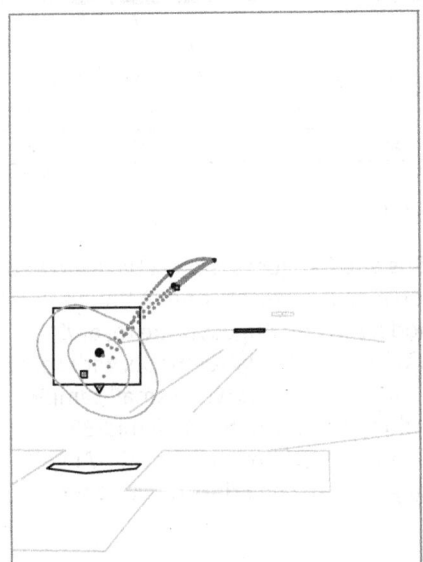	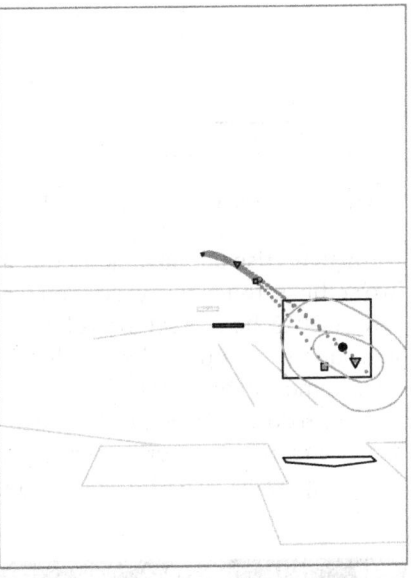

Type	Frequency	Velocity	H Movement	V Movement
● Fastball	50.4%	95.5 [109]	-4.8 [109]	-15.1 [102]
□ Sinker	11.9%	95.3 [114]	-14 [91]	-19.6 [103]
+ Cutter				
▲ Changeup				
× Splitter				
▽ Slider	37.4%	81.7 [89]	17.9 [154]	-35.9 [92]
◇ Curveball				
⊕ Slow Curveball				
✻ Knuckleball				
▼ Screwball				

Miguel Del Pozo LHP

Born: 10/14/92   Age: 27   Bats: L   Throws: L
Height: 6'1"   Weight: 180   Origin: International Free Agent, 2010

YEAR	TEAM	LVL	AGE	W	L	SV	G	GS	IP	H	HR	BB/9	K/9	K	GB%	BABIP
2017	JUP	A+	24	2	0	0	12	0	16^2	12	0	2.7	9.2	17	50%	.273
2018	JAX	AA	25	5	0	1	28	0	34	37	3	4.0	9.0	34	39%	.343
2019	NAS	AAA	26	2	3	1	38	0	45^2	53	5	4.1	12.8	65	37%	.432
2019	LAA	MLB	26	1	1	0	17	0	9^1	10	3	7.7	10.6	11	27%	.304
2020	PIT	MLB	27	2	2	0	33	0	35	33	6	4.4	8.7	34	36%	.281

Comparables: Adrian Houser, Steven Okert, Dustin Antolin

Through his rise up the ranks of the Marlins and Rangers systems, Del Pozo had two settings: too many walks, and *way* too many walks. At Triple-A Round Rock early in 2019, he was set to the former mode. After an August trade to, and subsequent call-up by, the Angels, he switched into the latter mode, with some extra home-run booster packs thrown in. Admittedly, this was a small sample, and Del Pozo is still a lefty whose whiff-inducing combination of a mid-90s heater and tumbling curve means that, though he was released by the Angels following the 2019 season, some team may want to keep tinkering under the hood.

YEAR	TEAM	LVL	AGE	WHIP	ERA	DRA	WARP	MPH	FB%	WHF	CSP
2017	JUP	A+	24	1.02	0.54	3.28	0.3				
2018	JAX	AA	25	1.53	3.97	5.30	-0.1				
2019	NAS	AAA	26	1.62	5.12	3.88	1.0				
2019	LAA	MLB	26	1.93	10.61	6.58	-0.1	96.2	56.8	11.5	44.2
2020	PIT	MLB	27	1.42	4.75	4.76	0.3	95.7	57.5	11.6	44.7

Miguel Del Pozo, continued

Pitch Shape vs LHH **Pitch Shape vs RHH**

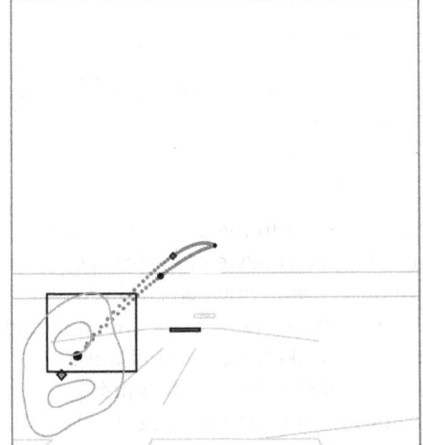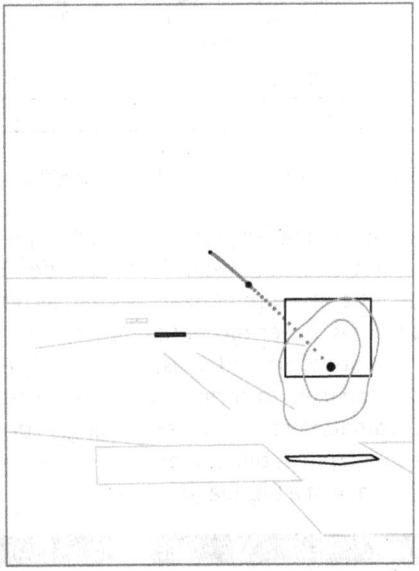

Type	Frequency	Velocity	H Movement	V Movement
● Fastball	56.8%	94.6 [106]	8.2 [94]	-13.5 [106]
☐ Sinker				
+ Cutter				
▲ Changeup	3.3%	88.1 [110]	16.1 [77]	-25.2 [106]
✕ Splitter				
▽ Slider				
◇ Curveball	39.9%	82.2 [112]	-3.8 [85]	-42.7 [110]
⊕ Slow Curveball				
✳ Knuckleball				
▼ Screwball				

Pirates Player Analysis - 55

Pittsburgh Pirates 2020

Robbie Erlin   LHP
Born: 10/08/90   Age: 29   Bats: R   Throws: L
Height: 6'0"   Weight: 190   Origin: Round 3, 2009 Draft (#93 overall)

YEAR	TEAM	LVL	AGE	W	L	SV	G	GS	IP	H	HR	BB/9	K/9	K	GB%	BABIP
2018	SDN	MLB	27	4	7	0	39	12	109	112	12	1.0	7.3	88	48%	.306
2019	ELP	AAA	28	0	1	1	10	0	15^1	26	2	1.2	8.2	14	51%	.453
2019	SDN	MLB	28	0	1	0	37	1	55^1	72	6	2.4	8.5	52	46%	.373
2020	SDN	MLB	29	2	2	0	33	0	35	38	5	2.2	7.7	30	46%	.313

Comparables: Erasmo Ramírez, Jaime García, Brett Anderson

A soft-tossing lefty junkballer, Erlin spent last summer in the bullpen handing out hits like Halloween SweeTarts before earning his release at season's end. His peripherals weren't nearly as bad as his run prevention, however, as Erlin posted a career-high strikeout rate while keeping his walk rate low and inducing his share of ground balls. He's exactly the type of strike-thrower that Dave Duncan used to sprinkle with pixie dust and sinker shavings, as he gifts Cardinals fans another surprisingly successful starter reclamation. Erlin has enough pitchability to be a useful swingman, and could yet carve out a role at the back of a big-league rotation.

YEAR	TEAM	LVL	AGE	WHIP	ERA	DRA	WARP	MPH	FB%	WHF	CSP
2018	SDN	MLB	27	1.14	4.21	3.05	2.6	92.3	59.2	10.3	52
2019	ELP	AAA	28	1.83	8.80	5.83	0.1				
2019	SDN	MLB	28	1.57	5.37	5.17	0.1	92.1	50.7	11.3	46.3
2020	SDN	MLB	29	1.34	4.65	4.65	0.3	91.6	55.5	10.7	48.8

Robbie Erlin, continued

Pitch Shape vs LHH

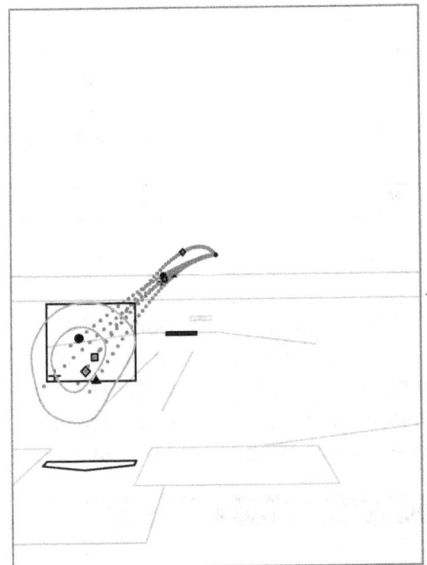

Pitch Shape vs RHH

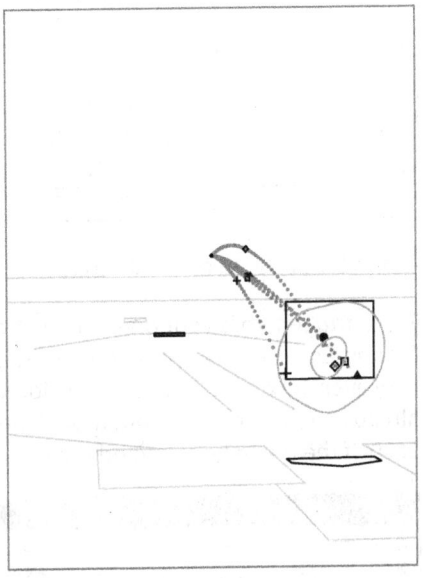

Type	Frequency	Velocity	H Movement	V Movement
● Fastball	29.7%	91 [96]	6.3 [103]	-13.9 [105]
□ Sinker	21.0%	90.7 [90]	12.9 [98]	-18.4 [107]
+ Cutter	10.1%	88.8 [100]	-0.8 [94]	-22.4 [106]
▲ Changeup	16.7%	83.6 [94]	8.4 [113]	-27.1 [101]
✕ Splitter				
▽ Slider				
◇ Curveball	22.0%	76.5 [93]	-4 [86]	-57.3 [80]
⊕ Slow Curveball				
✳ Knuckleball				
▼ Screwball				

Luis Escobar RHP

Born: 05/30/96 Age: 24 Bats: R Throws: R
Height: 6'1" Weight: 205 Origin: International Free Agent, 2013

YEAR	TEAM	LVL	AGE	W	L	SV	G	GS	IP	H	HR	BB/9	K/9	K	GB%	BABIP
2017	WVA	A	21	10	7	0	26	25	131^2	97	9	4.1	11.5	168	44%	.282
2018	BRD	A+	22	7	6	0	17	16	92^2	76	9	3.7	8.3	85	48%	.272
2018	ALT	AA	22	4	0	0	7	7	35^2	30	4	5.3	6.3	25	43%	.248
2019	BRD	A+	23	0	0	3	10	0	13^1	6	0	4.1	10.1	15	58%	.194
2019	IND	AAA	23	2	1	1	24	5	55	54	7	5.2	9.3	57	48%	.329
2019	PIT	MLB	23	0	0	0	4	0	5^2	10	1	6.4	3.2	2	46%	.429
2020	PIT	MLB	24	2	2	0	33	0	35	41	7	5.1	7.3	28	43%	.317

Comparables: Merandy Gonzalez, Dylan Cease, Kendry Flores

The *Cartagenero* is your big-stuff pitcher with control issues *du jour* for the Pirates. Escobar has a primetime fastball with life and a real-deal curve, but his very eventful delivery causes the aforementioned sloppy geography. He's already a reliever as a result, though he should get more big-league duty come 2020. If the K rate ticks up and the walk rate ticks down, he could be fun.

YEAR	TEAM	LVL	AGE	WHIP	ERA	DRA	WARP	MPH	FB%	WHF	CSP
2017	WVA	A	21	1.19	3.83	3.42	2.9				
2018	BRD	A+	22	1.23	3.98	4.04	1.4				
2018	ALT	AA	22	1.43	4.54	5.21	0.1				
2019	BRD	A+	23	0.90	0.00	3.34	0.2				
2019	IND	AAA	23	1.56	4.09	5.36	0.6				
2019	PIT	MLB	23	2.47	7.94	4.72	0.0	96.6	68.3	9.6	45.5
2020	PIT	MLB	24	1.75	6.74	6.18	-0.3	96.4	70.3	9.9	46.9

Luis Escobar, continued

Pitch Shape vs LHH
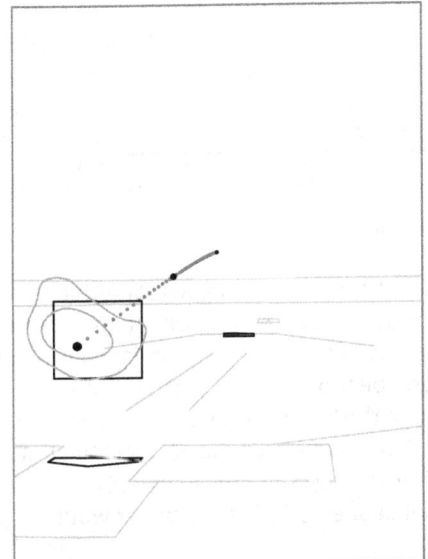

Pitch Shape vs RHH
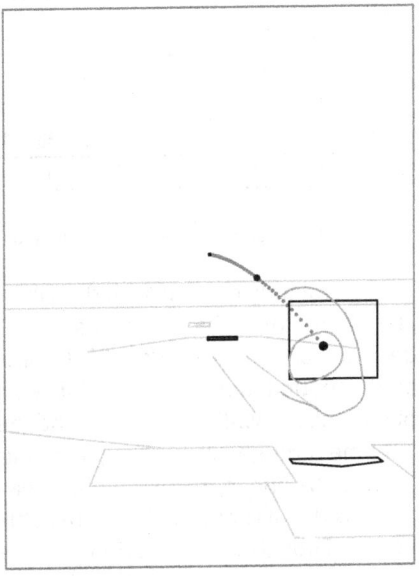

Type	Frequency	Velocity	H Movement	V Movement
● Fastball	68.3%	95.1 [108]	-10.1 [86]	-13.9 [105]
☐ Sinker				
+ Cutter				
▲ Changeup	19.2%	84.3 [96]	-9.6 [108]	-24.9 [107]
✕ Splitter				
▽ Slider				
◇ Curveball	12.5%	78.7 [100]	10.3 [112]	-45.4 [105]
⊕ Slow Curveball				
✳ Knuckleball				
▼ Screwball				

Pittsburgh Pirates 2020

Michael Feliz RHP

Born: 06/28/93 Age: 27 Bats: R Throws: R
Height: 6'4" Weight: 240 Origin: International Free Agent, 2010

YEAR	TEAM	LVL	AGE	W	L	SV	G	GS	IP	H	HR	BB/9	K/9	K	GB%	BABIP
2017	HOU	MLB	24	4	2	0	46	0	48	53	8	4.1	13.1	70	31%	.381
2018	IND	AAA	25	2	1	2	9	0	10	13	2	0.9	10.8	12	40%	.393
2018	PIT	MLB	25	1	2	0	47	0	47²	49	6	4.3	10.4	55	33%	.331
2019	IND	AAA	26	0	0	2	10	0	15	13	1	4.2	13.2	22	37%	.353
2019	PIT	MLB	26	4	4	0	58	1	56¹	44	11	4.3	11.7	73	38%	.262
2020	PIT	MLB	27	3	3	2	57	0	60	50	9	4.1	11.4	76	36%	.291

Comparables: Adrian Houser, John Gant, Domingo Germán

You're probably familiar with the Tik Tok-featured song that goes something like, ahem, "don't be suspicious…don't be suspicious" and so on. (If not, ask the designated teenager in your life for assistance.) Feliz mutters a similar command on the mound: don't be too hittable…don't be too hittable. He strikes out a lot of batters, but walks a lot, too—and, despite the K rate, he's yielded 1.5 homers per nine through 225 big-league innings. It seems overzealous to conclude that he's maybe one more hit per nine away from being out of the league, yet our guess is that if that were to happen, his subsequent big-league career wouldn't be long enough to put in a bun.

YEAR	TEAM	LVL	AGE	WHIP	ERA	DRA	WARP	MPH	FB%	WHF	CSP
2017	HOU	MLB	24	1.56	5.62	3.18	1.1	98.6	71.9	15.4	50.4
2018	IND	AAA	25	1.40	7.20	5.76	-0.1				
2018	PIT	MLB	25	1.51	5.66	5.20	-0.1	97.8	73.6	11	46.1
2019	IND	AAA	26	1.33	1.20	3.11	0.5				
2019	PIT	MLB	26	1.26	3.99	3.38	1.2	97.6	73.4	13.6	46.3
2020	PIT	MLB	27	1.29	3.88	4.00	0.9	97.4	74	13.3	47.8

Michael Feliz, continued

Pitch Shape vs LHH

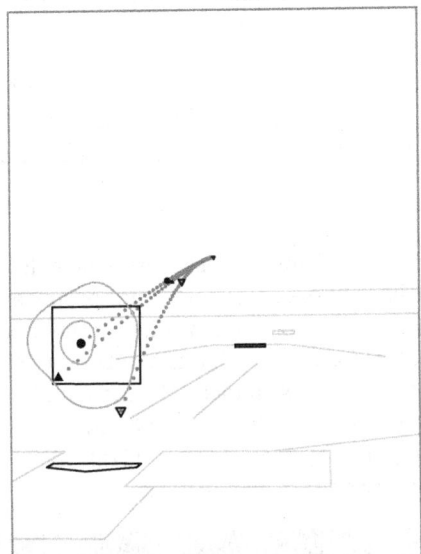

Pitch Shape vs RHH

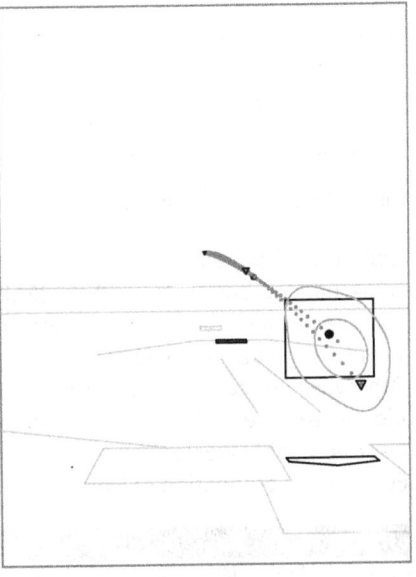

Type	Frequency	Velocity	H Movement	V Movement
● Fastball	73.4%	95.4 [108]	-1.7 [123]	-11 [113]
□ Sinker				
+ Cutter				
▲ Changeup	6.4%	86.4 [104]	-9.6 [108]	-20.1 [121]
✕ Splitter				
▽ Slider	20.2%	82 [90]	7.5 [111]	-33.1 [100]
◇ Curveball				
✦ Slow Curveball				
✱ Knuckleball				
▼ Screwball				

Pittsburgh Pirates 2020

Derek Holland   LHP

Born: 10/09/86 Age: 33 Bats: B Throws: L
Height: 6'2" Weight: 213 Origin: Round 25, 2006 Draft (#748 overall)

YEAR	TEAM	LVL	AGE	W	L	SV	G	GS	IP	H	HR	BB/9	K/9	K	GB%	BABIP
2017	CHA	MLB	30	7	14	0	29	26	135	156	31	5.0	6.9	104	39%	.307
2018	SFN	MLB	31	7	9	0	36	30	171^1	154	19	3.5	8.9	169	42%	.288
2019	CHN	MLB	32	0	1	0	20	1	15^2	14	3	5.7	6.3	11	38%	.250
2019	SFN	MLB	32	2	4	0	31	7	68^2	68	17	4.6	9.3	71	45%	.282
2020	CHN	MLB	33	2	2	0	33	0	35	36	6	3.9	8.6	33	42%	.305

Comparables: John Danks, Brett Cecil, Sterling Hitchcock

Holland is about as friendly to lefties as Mitch McConnell. Last season, he held same-handed batters to a .192/.286/.242 slash line, suggesting he has promise as a specialist of some kind—whatever that does or doesn't look like in the new world. That's about the long and short of the positives we have to note here. Otherwise, his season was so poor as to endanger his chances of a sustained big-league career. His impersonation of a big-league starter was particularly poor—arguably worse than his impersonation of Harry Caray, or, at least, Will Ferrell's impersonation of Harry Caray, because that's all it really is.

YEAR	TEAM	LVL	AGE	WHIP	ERA	DRA	WARP	MPH	FB%	WHF	CSP
2017	CHA	MLB	30	1.71	6.20	8.59	-4.6	93.4	55.1	7.8	45.1
2018	SFN	MLB	31	1.29	3.57	3.80	2.9	93.8	56.9	11.2	49.5
2019	CHN	MLB	32	1.53	6.89	2.52	0.5	95.3	67.4	9.6	46.4
2019	SFN	MLB	32	1.50	5.90	6.96	-1.1	94.7	60.9	12.5	47.8
2020	CHN	MLB	33	1.46	5.04	5.03	0.2	92.9	57.1	10.3	47

Derek Holland, continued

Pitch Shape vs LHH

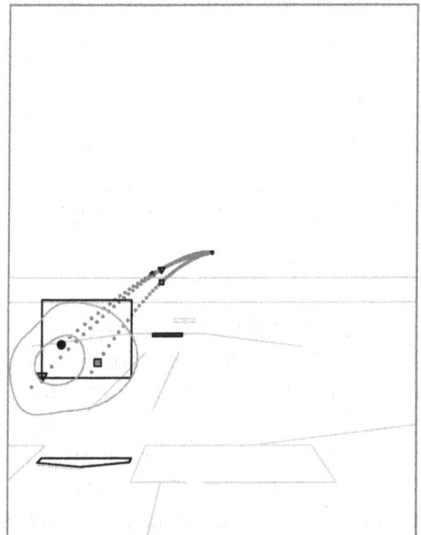

Pitch Shape vs RHH

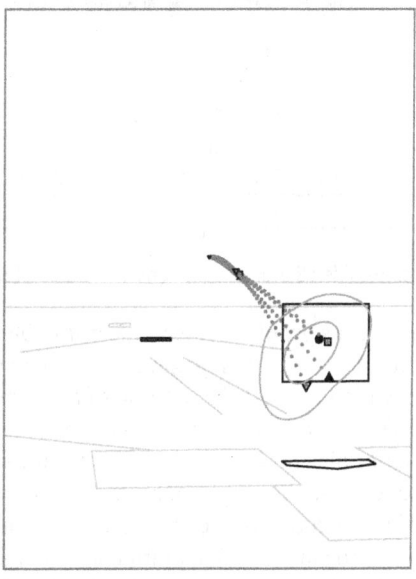

Type	Frequency	Velocity	H Movement	V Movement
● Fastball	32.2%	92.3 [100]	12.4 [75]	-15.4 [101]
☐ Sinker	29.9%	93.1 [103]	14.8 [86]	-17.6 [110]
+ Cutter				
▲ Changeup	3.8%	84.2 [96]	10.4 [104]	-24.1 [110]
✕ Splitter				
▽ Slider	33.5%	81.1 [86]	1 [75]	-33.7 [98]
◇ Curveball				
⊕ Slow Curveball				
✱ Knuckleball				
▼ Screwball				

Pittsburgh Pirates 2020

Sam Howard   LHP
Born: 03/05/93   Age: 27   Bats: R   Throws: L
Height: 6'3"   Weight: 170   Origin: Round 3, 2014 Draft (#82 overall)

YEAR	TEAM	LVL	AGE	W	L	SV	G	GS	IP	H	HR	BB/9	K/9	K	GB%	BABIP
2017	HFD	AA	24	1	4	0	9	9	46^1	31	5	1.9	7.8	40	39%	.208
2017	ABQ	AAA	24	4	4	0	15	14	81	82	6	3.7	7.1	64	41%	.309
2018	ABQ	AAA	25	3	8	0	21	21	96	106	13	3.2	7.5	80	40%	.327
2018	COL	MLB	25	0	0	0	4	0	4	5	0	6.8	2.2	1	53%	.333
2019	ABQ	AAA	26	4	1	1	42	0	50^2	50	5	4.1	11.0	62	44%	.363
2019	COL	MLB	26	2	0	0	20	0	19	21	5	4.7	10.9	23	42%	.320
2020	PIT	MLB	27	1	1	0	23	0	24	20	4	3.8	9.0	24	40%	.268

Comparables: Steven Brault, Harrison Musgrave, Brian Johnson

Howard's problem wasn't his home park, like so many of his peers. Just three of the 14 earned runs he gave up came in Colorado. Quality lineups were his downfall instead. All but one of the remaining earned runs on his ledger came on the road, courtesy of three of the better offenses in baseball: the Dodgers, Nationals and Astros. Perhaps it's not surprising that the lefty's combination of solid-yet-unspectacular stuff and pitchability plays better against mediocre offenses than good ones. Perhaps it's just a small sample size fluke that his OPS allowed was over 500 points higher against teams with a winning record than against those who were sub-.500. For the first time in his career, Howard was exclusively a reliever, and it took him a little while to start leaning on the slider more heavily. The strikeouts certainly went up once he did, even if the results didn't match the peripherals. He ditched the lackluster change (Howard threw just six all season), and when he did locate the slider, hitters had real trouble with it. There might not be enough here for a great bullpen arm, but he has the potential to make a solid middle reliever.

YEAR	TEAM	LVL	AGE	WHIP	ERA	DRA	WARP	MPH	FB%	WHF	CSP
2017	HFD	AA	24	0.88	2.33	2.54	1.5				
2017	ABQ	AAA	24	1.42	3.89	3.82	1.6				
2018	ABQ	AAA	25	1.46	5.06	4.99	0.6				
2018	COL	MLB	25	2.00	2.25	8.49	-0.2	92.7	48.8	8.1	50.2
2019	ABQ	AAA	26	1.44	3.91	3.01	1.6				
2019	COL	MLB	26	1.63	6.63	3.91	0.3	94.0	44.1	15.4	43
2020	PIT	MLB	27	1.28	3.89	4.07	0.4	93.3	45.4	14.5	46.7

Sam Howard, continued

Pitch Shape vs LHH

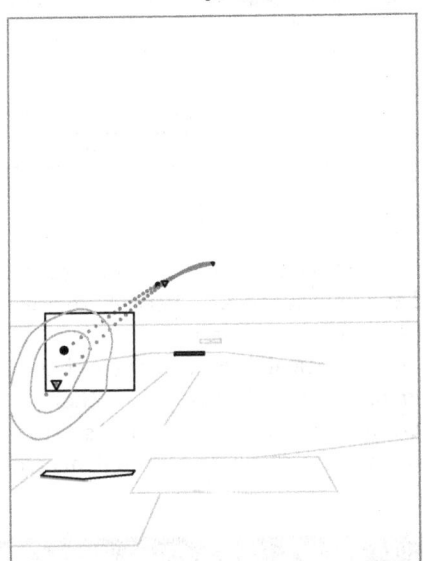

Pitch Shape vs RHH

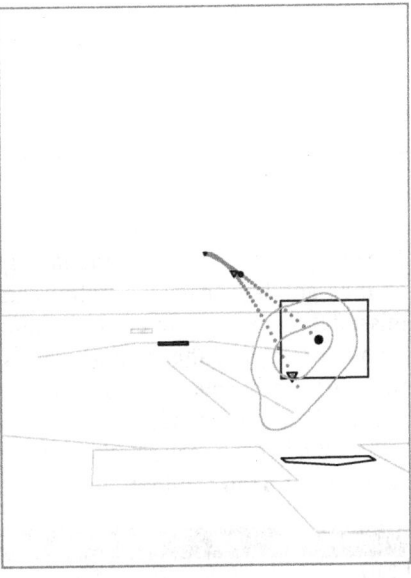

Type	Frequency	Velocity	H Movement	V Movement
● Fastball	44.1%	92.5 [100]	5.5 [106]	-13.4 [107]
☐ Sinker				
+ Cutter				
▲ Changeup				
✕ Splitter				
▽ Slider	55.9%	84.9 [102]	-2.4 [89]	-29.6 [110]
◇ Curveball				
✦ Slow Curveball				
✳ Knuckleball				
▼ Screwball				

Pittsburgh Pirates 2020

Keone Kela RHP

Born: 04/16/93 Age: 27 Bats: R Throws: R
Height: 6'1" Weight: 210 Origin: Round 12, 2012 Draft (#396 overall)

YEAR	TEAM	LVL	AGE	W	L	SV	G	GS	IP	H	HR	BB/9	K/9	K	GB%	BABIP
2017	TEX	MLB	24	4	1	2	39	0	38^2	18	4	4.0	11.9	51	32%	.179
2018	TEX	MLB	25	3	3	24	38	0	36^2	28	3	3.4	10.8	44	40%	.275
2018	PIT	MLB	25	0	1	0	16	0	15^1	10	2	2.9	12.9	22	27%	.258
2019	PIT	MLB	26	2	0	1	32	0	29^2	19	3	3.3	10.0	33	36%	.225
2020	PIT	MLB	27	3	3	23	57	0	60	48	8	3.8	10.8	72	38%	.280

Comparables: Bruce Rondón, Neftalí Feliz, Cam Bedrosian

The best way to beat Kela's menacing fastball-curve combination is to catch him on the right day. Absences, both excused and unexcused, are everywhere. He missed three months to elbow inflammation; he also took a 10-game mandatory hiatus after that wild Reds-Pirates physical disagreement for being the one to throw over a batter's head; *and*, remarkably, he had yet another suspension, that one team-enforced for clashing with a coach. Kela was virtually unhittable in the second half, but his greatest enemy is himself (though his arm seems to be a tad self-loathing as well).

YEAR	TEAM	LVL	AGE	WHIP	ERA	DRA	WARP	MPH	FB%	WHF	CSP
2017	TEX	MLB	24	0.91	2.79	4.75	0.2	98.5	57.9	12.2	49.6
2018	TEX	MLB	25	1.15	3.44	3.50	0.6	99.0	64.3	12.7	49.5
2018	PIT	MLB	25	0.98	2.93	2.37	0.5	98.7	58.7	16.1	50.3
2019	PIT	MLB	26	1.01	2.12	3.83	0.5	98.2	53.5	11.7	46.7
2020	PIT	MLB	27	1.24	3.60	3.79	1.1	98.1	59.3	12.8	49

Keone Kela, continued

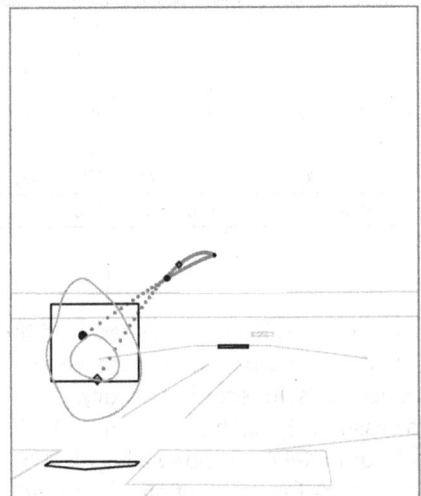

Pitch Shape vs LHH

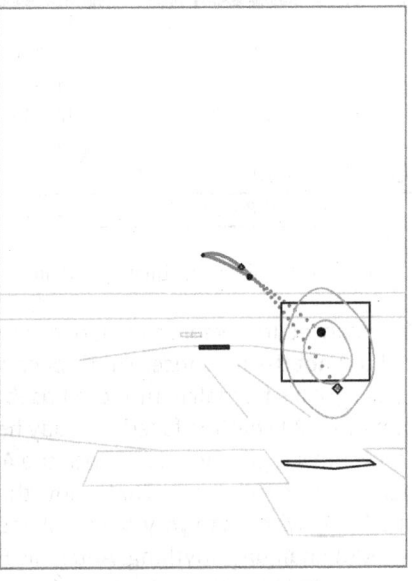

Pitch Shape vs RHH

Type	Frequency	Velocity	H Movement	V Movement
● Fastball	53.5%	96.6 [112]	-3.1 [117]	-10.6 [114]
☐ Sinker				
+ Cutter				
▲ Changeup				
✕ Splitter				
▽ Slider				
◇ Curveball	43.7%	82.1 [112]	1.9 [77]	-41.7 [112]
✦ Slow Curveball				
✳ Knuckleball				
▼ Screwball				

Mitch Keller   RHP

Born: 04/04/96   Age: 24   Bats: R   Throws: R
Height: 6'2"   Weight: 210   Origin: Round 2, 2014 Draft (#64 overall)

YEAR	TEAM	LVL	AGE	W	L	SV	G	GS	IP	H	HR	BB/9	K/9	K	GB%	BABIP
2017	BRD	A+	21	6	3	0	15	15	77^1	57	5	2.3	7.4	64	55%	.248
2017	ALT	AA	21	2	2	0	6	6	34^2	25	2	2.9	11.7	45	48%	.280
2018	ALT	AA	22	9	2	0	14	14	86	64	7	3.3	8.0	76	55%	.251
2018	IND	AAA	22	3	2	0	10	10	52^1	59	3	3.8	9.8	57	35%	.366
2019	IND	AAA	23	7	5	0	19	19	103^2	94	9	3.0	10.7	123	46%	.315
2019	PIT	MLB	23	1	5	0	11	11	48	72	6	3.0	12.2	65	41%	.475
2020	PIT	MLB	24	7	7	0	23	23	113	108	13	3.3	10.0	127	43%	.315

Comparables: Jake Faria, Zack Littell, Lucas Sims

After consecutive years as one of our top 20 prospects, Keller finally received the call but not the response. That's because of either the worst luck or the worst tipping of his fastball in modern baseball. Check this. In recorded history, minimum 200 batters faced, nobody had a seasonal BABIP higher than .432 (Tim Lincecum's regrettable 2016 with the Angels) until Keller dropped a big ol' .475 right there for all to see. That's now the benchmark for standing on the mound and being witness to your own horror show. He's likely to be better this year without changing anything. And if his BABIP does, somehow, go up? Then he needs to tell his catcher to stop whispering to the batter, "wowie, watch this next fastball, it's the cat's pajamas," (or whatever catchers say these days) because that's the only explanation that makes sense for his struggles.

YEAR	TEAM	LVL	AGE	WHIP	ERA	DRA	WARP	MPH	FB%	WHF	CSP
2017	BRD	A+	21	1.00	3.14	3.14	1.9				
2017	ALT	AA	21	1.04	3.12	2.41	1.1				
2018	ALT	AA	22	1.12	2.72	3.55	1.8				
2018	IND	AAA	22	1.55	4.82	6.93	-0.8				
2019	IND	AAA	23	1.24	3.56	3.38	3.3				
2019	PIT	MLB	23	1.83	7.12	4.18	0.8	97.5	59.5	13.7	47.8
2020	PIT	MLB	24	1.32	4.00	4.12	2.1	97.3	61.3	14.1	49.3

Mitch Keller, continued

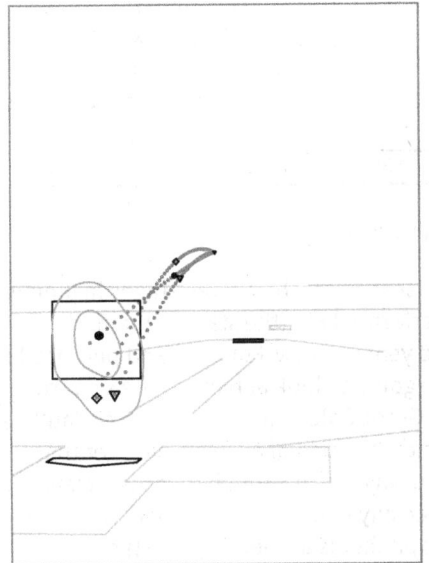
Pitch Shape vs LHH

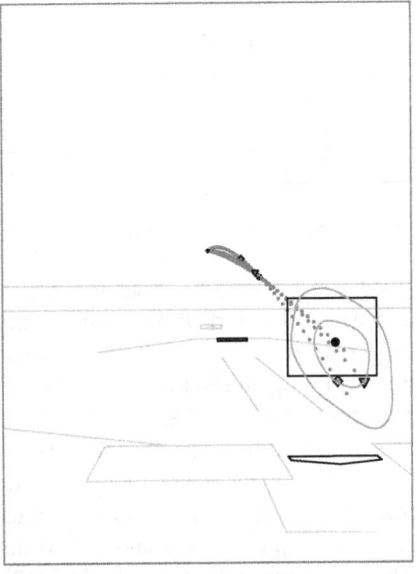
Pitch Shape vs RHH

Type	Frequency	Velocity	H Movement	V Movement
● Fastball	59.5%	95.5 [109]	-5.5 [106]	-12.7 [108]
☐ Sinker				
+ Cutter				
▲ Changeup	3.7%	91.2 [121]	-12 [96]	-20.8 [119]
✕ Splitter				
▽ Slider	20.8%	87.8 [114]	4 [96]	-30.8 [107]
◇ Curveball	15.9%	81.2 [109]	8.6 [105]	-49.8 [95]
⊕ Slow Curveball				
✱ Knuckleball				
▼ Screwball				

Joe Musgrove RHP

Born: 12/04/92 Age: 27 Bats: R Throws: R
Height: 6'5" Weight: 230 Origin: Round 1, 2011 Draft (#46 overall)

YEAR	TEAM	LVL	AGE	W	L	SV	G	GS	IP	H	HR	BB/9	K/9	K	GB%	BABIP
2017	FRE	AAA	24	1	0	0	1	1	7	1	0	2.6	9.0	7	54%	.077
2017	HOU	MLB	24	7	8	2	38	15	109^1	117	18	2.3	8.1	98	46%	.316
2018	IND	AAA	25	1	1	0	2	2	10^2	10	0	1.7	9.3	11	41%	.312
2018	PIT	MLB	25	6	9	0	19	19	115^1	113	12	1.8	7.8	100	48%	.294
2019	PIT	MLB	26	11	12	0	32	31	170^1	168	21	2.1	8.3	157	45%	.299
2020	PIT	MLB	27	9	9	0	28	28	149	143	20	2.3	8.3	138	44%	.293

Comparables: Jameson Taillon, James Shields, Yonny Chirinos

Musgrove is a solid No. 4 starter who last season reached career-highs in innings and strikeouts, and who markedly outperformed FIP (the starting pitcher's mirror, mirror on the wall) for the second year in a row. For now, and perhaps for however long he's in Pittsburgh, fans are going to look at him as if he's sporting a tattoo that reads "Yes, I was traded for Gerrit Cole." First off, it's not his fault he was the positional counterpart in that trade. Second of all, why even get that tattoo, unless this is a *Memento* situation? Anyway, it's tough to disassociate from the player you were traded for, especially when said disembarking player is a top-five pitcher and said onboarding pitcher is a "mere" No. 4 starter (though he was top-30 by DRA in 2019). But one great piece of advice is to learn to let go; another is to be happy that the Pirates haven't turned the No. 4 they received for their No. 1 into a No. 7 with a large drink.

YEAR	TEAM	LVL	AGE	WHIP	ERA	DRA	WARP	MPH	FB%	WHF	CSP
2017	FRE	AAA	24	0.43	0.00	2.94	0.2				
2017	HOU	MLB	24	1.33	4.77	4.49	1.2	96.1	48	13	51.6
2018	IND	AAA	25	1.12	5.06	3.79	0.2				
2018	PIT	MLB	25	1.18	4.06	3.43	2.5	95.5	50.3	12.5	53.5
2019	PIT	MLB	26	1.22	4.44	3.59	4.0	94.7	49.5	12.7	49
2020	PIT	MLB	27	1.22	3.85	4.07	2.9	94.7	50	12.9	51.8

Joe Musgrove, continued

Pitch Shape vs LHH

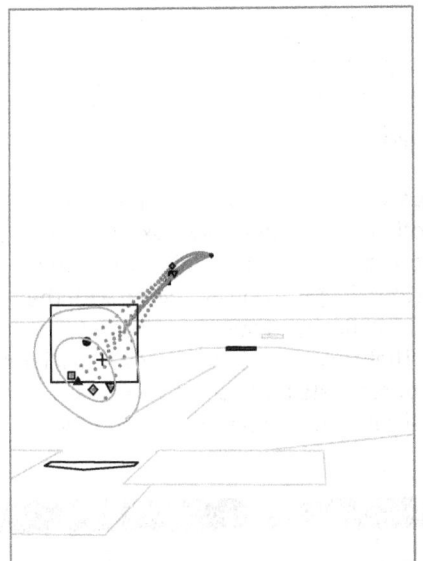

Pitch Shape vs RHH

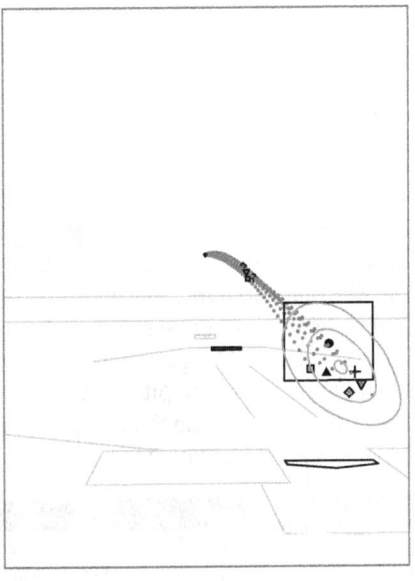

Type	Frequency	Velocity	H Movement	V Movement
● Fastball	37.9%	92.9 [101]	-4.1 [112]	-17 [97]
□ Sinker	11.6%	91.8 [96]	-9 [123]	-23.2 [90]
+ Cutter	8.4%	88.9 [102]	3.2 [108]	-24.2 [100]
▲ Changeup	10.6%	85.5 [101]	-5.8 [125]	-28.4 [97]
✕ Splitter				
▽ Slider	22.4%	83.4 [96]	10.5 [123]	-34.9 [95]
◇ Curveball	9.2%	82.1 [112]	6.6 [96]	-45.3 [105]
⊕ Slow Curveball				
✳ Knuckleball				
▼ Screwball				

Héctor Noesí   RHP
Born: 01/26/87   Age: 33   Bats: R   Throws: R
Height: 6'3"   Weight: 205   Origin: International Free Agent, 2004

YEAR	TEAM	LVL	AGE	W	L	SV	G	GS	IP	H	HR	BB/9	K/9	K	GB%	BABIP
2019	NWO	AAA	32	11	4	0	21	21	125	112	27	2.2	9.6	133	41%	.271
2019	MIA	MLB	32	0	3	0	12	4	27^2	30	7	4.6	7.8	24	33%	.295
2020	PIT	MLB	33	2	2	0	33	0	35	36	7	3.1	8.0	31	37%	.289

Comparables: Luis Cessa, Jason Bergmann, Chris Stratton

The curse conferred onto Noesí and Jesús Montero in 2012 when they were dealt to Seattle may have paid Noesí another visit, as new laws taxing foreign players in the Korean Baseball Organization apparently compelled Noesí and the Kia Tigers to part ways before 2019. Noesí had previously starred with the Tigers, winning 46 games and posting a 3.79 ERA over three seasons and winning the 2017 league championship. That success didn't carry over to Miami, where the 32-year-old pitcher struggled to replicate the mediocrity of his previous major league tenure. He can still eat some innings, but any utility beyond that starts with an "F".

YEAR	TEAM	LVL	AGE	WHIP	ERA	DRA	WARP	MPH	FB%	WHF	CSP
2019	NWO	AAA	32	1.14	3.82	3.21	4.2				
2019	MIA	MLB	32	1.59	8.46	6.58	-0.3	94.8	44.1	13.3	46.3
2020	PIT	MLB	33	1.38	5.06	5.15	0.1	93.8	43.5	13.1	45.8

Héctor Noesi, continued

Pitch Shape vs LHH

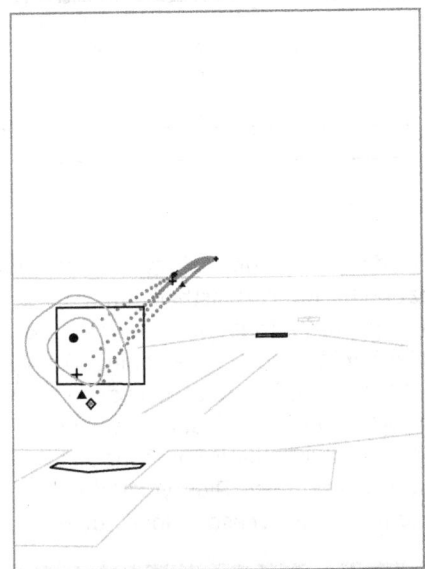

Pitch Shape vs RHH

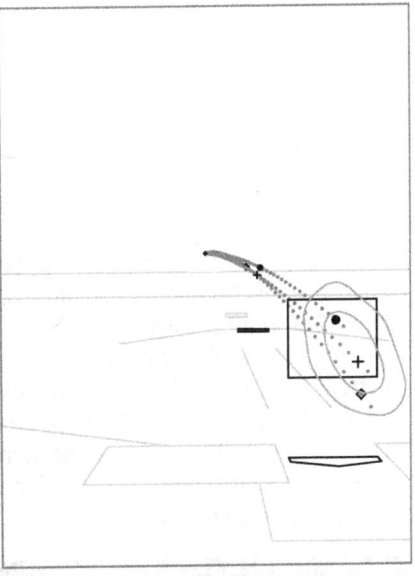

Type	Frequency	Velocity	H Movement	V Movement
● Fastball	43.9%	93.2 [102]	-10.6 [83]	-15.9 [100]
☐ Sinker				
+ Cutter	29.8%	88.4 [99]	0.3 [91]	-23.4 [103]
▲ Changeup	9.5%	86.3 [104]	-13.3 [90]	-25.9 [105]
✕ Splitter				
▽ Slider				
◇ Curveball	16.7%	80.3 [106]	5.5 [92]	-41.9 [112]
✛ Slow Curveball				
✱ Knuckleball				
▼ Screwball				

Richard Rodríguez RHP

Born: 03/04/90 Age: 30 Bats: R Throws: R
Height: 6'4" Weight: 230 Origin: International Free Agent, 2010

YEAR	TEAM	LVL	AGE	W	L	SV	G	GS	IP	H	HR	BB/9	K/9	K	GB%	BABIP
2017	NOR	AAA	27	4	4	10	42	1	70^2	56	5	2.3	10.2	80	29%	.285
2017	BAL	MLB	27	0	0	0	5	0	5^2	12	4	4.8	4.8	3	46%	.400
2018	PIT	MLB	28	4	3	0	63	0	69^1	55	5	2.5	11.4	88	40%	.309
2019	PIT	MLB	29	4	5	1	72	0	65^1	65	14	3.2	8.7	63	44%	.280
2020	PIT	MLB	30	3	3	5	57	0	60	59	11	3.0	9.3	62	40%	.300

Comparables: Ben Rowen, Josh Lueke, Paul Sewald

Modern analytics have more or less replaced celestial numerology in sports, but consider: in his breakout 2018, Rodríguez and his low-90s fastball didn't allow a run in 17 straight games. In '19, he had a 19-game shutout appearance streak. Most of us can look at this and say, good for him, but no way he's going to have 22 straight shutout relief appearances in 2020. It's very hard to do in general, and especially for a pitcher equipped with a low-90s fastball and a declining strikeout rate. But there has to be some space left in athletic competition to believe that weird things can happen in radical sequence. Plus, you didn't have much of a reason to watch Rodríguez heading into the season. Now? You do.

YEAR	TEAM	LVL	AGE	WHIP	ERA	DRA	WARP	MPH	FB%	WHF	CSP
2017	NOR	AAA	27	1.05	2.42	3.06	1.7				
2017	BAL	MLB	27	2.65	14.29	8.32	-0.2	95.1	65.8	6.7	50.2
2018	PIT	MLB	28	1.07	2.47	2.82	1.7	94.9	75.1	15.2	50.7
2019	PIT	MLB	29	1.35	3.72	4.70	0.5	95.0	85.2	11.6	48
2020	PIT	MLB	30	1.32	4.56	4.69	0.5	94.2	80	12.9	49.3

Richard Rodríguez, continued

Pitch Shape vs LHH

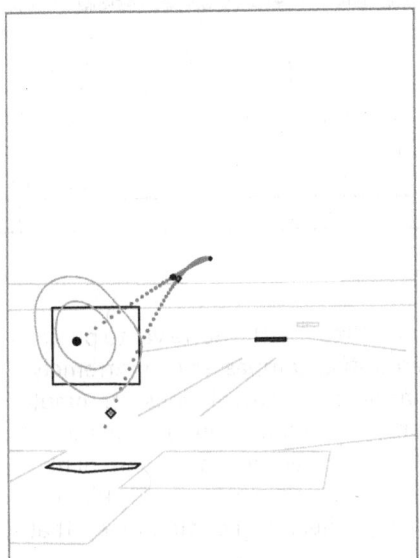

Pitch Shape vs RHH

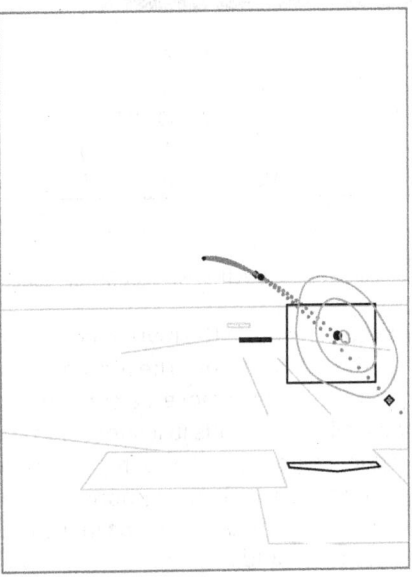

Type	Frequency	Velocity	H Movement	V Movement
● Fastball	85.0%	93.5 [103]	-11.9 [78]	-14.7 [103]
☐ Sinker				
+ Cutter				
▲ Changeup				
✕ Splitter				
▽ Slider				
◇ Curveball	14.3%	81.9 [111]	5.1 [91]	-40.6 [115]
⊕ Slow Curveball				
✱ Knuckleball				
▼ Screwball				

Chris Stratton   RHP

Born: 08/22/90   Age: 29   Bats: R   Throws: R
Height: 6'2"   Weight: 211   Origin: Round 1, 2012 Draft (#20 overall)

YEAR	TEAM	LVL	AGE	W	L	SV	G	GS	IP	H	HR	BB/9	K/9	K	GB%	BABIP
2017	SAC	AAA	26	4	5	0	15	15	79^1	94	10	2.5	8.1	71	53%	.340
2017	SFN	MLB	26	4	4	1	13	10	58^2	59	5	4.3	7.8	51	46%	.316
2018	SAC	AAA	27	3	0	0	4	4	24	25	3	3.0	9.0	24	44%	.324
2018	SFN	MLB	27	10	10	0	28	26	145	153	19	3.4	7.0	112	44%	.306
2019	PIT	MLB	28	1	1	0	28	0	46^2	50	7	2.9	9.1	47	39%	.328
2019	LAA	MLB	28	0	2	0	7	5	29^1	43	6	5.5	6.8	22	43%	.378
2020	PIT	MLB	29	2	2	0	45	0	48	50	7	3.6	7.7	41	43%	.305

Comparables: Drew VerHagen, Cody Martin, Sam Gaviglio

Stratton is among the myriad go-getters with Great Stuff who've yet to put it all together for a season. The aforementioned stuff encompasses two extremely spinny secondary moves: a curve that spins over 3,000 revolutions per minute, and a slider that falls just short of that mark. (That's fourth and 12th in the league, respectively.) Alas, his stint in the Angels rotation was a month of his getting spun around by opponents, and he finished the season in the Pirates bullpen, turning over lineups in a multi-inning relief role. For our money, that's where he should remain.

YEAR	TEAM	LVL	AGE	WHIP	ERA	DRA	WARP	MPH	FB%	WHF	CSP
2017	SAC	AAA	26	1.46	5.11	4.50	1.0				
2017	SFN	MLB	26	1.48	3.68	4.62	0.6	93.7	62.4	9.9	45.5
2018	SAC	AAA	27	1.38	3.00	4.40	0.3				
2018	SFN	MLB	27	1.43	5.09	4.99	0.5	93.2	62.2	9.6	49.9
2019	PIT	MLB	28	1.39	3.66	4.55	0.5	94.9	63.7	13.2	47.9
2019	LAA	MLB	28	2.08	8.59	8.60	-1.0	92.8	46.7	9.5	44.4
2020	PIT	MLB	29	1.44	4.73	4.78	0.3	92.9	60.5	10.4	47.4

Chris Stratton, continued

Pitch Shape vs LHH

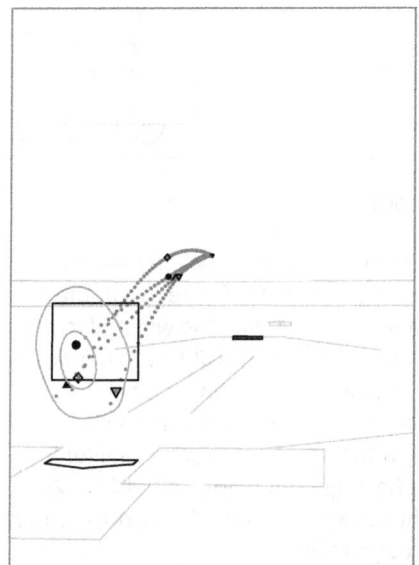

Pitch Shape vs RHH

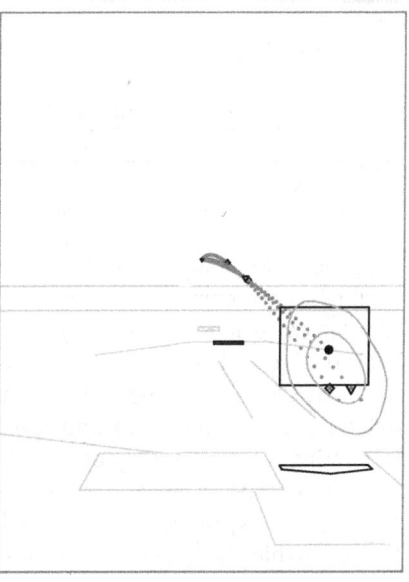

Type	Frequency	Velocity	H Movement	V Movement
● Fastball	56.9%	92.6 [100]	-4.6 [110]	-14.9 [103]
☐ Sinker				
+ Cutter				
▲ Changeup	5.9%	85.3 [100]	-12.1 [96]	-28.1 [98]
✕ Splitter				
▽ Slider	24.5%	84.8 [102]	6.1 [105]	-35.1 [94]
◇ Curveball	12.7%	77.5 [96]	15.7 [133]	-50.8 [93]
⊕ Slow Curveball				
✱ Knuckleball				
▼ Screwball				

Pirates Player Analysis - 77

Jameson Taillon RHP

Born: 11/18/91 Age: 28 Bats: R Throws: R
Height: 6'5" Weight: 230 Origin: Round 1, 2010 Draft (#2 overall)

YEAR	TEAM	LVL	AGE	W	L	SV	G	GS	IP	H	HR	BB/9	K/9	K	GB%	BABIP
2017	IND	AAA	25	0	1	0	2	2	11	12	0	1.6	12.3	15	58%	.387
2017	PIT	MLB	25	8	7	0	25	25	133^2	152	11	3.1	8.4	125	49%	.352
2018	PIT	MLB	26	14	10	0	32	32	191	179	20	2.2	8.4	179	48%	.298
2019	PIT	MLB	27	2	3	0	7	7	37^1	34	4	1.9	7.2	30	51%	.272
2020	PIT	MLB	28	2	2	0	33	0	35	34	4	2.5	8.2	32	48%	.296

Comparables: Joe Musgrove, James Shields, Ricky Nolasco

Best known for being drafted after Bryce Harper and before Manny Machado, Taillon has overcome a lot of adversity during his career—to the extent that slipping twice under the Tommy John knife somehow isn't the worst of it, even if it is the latest. There's no questioning his resiliency or his ability to bounce back—he's Flubber-esque in that regard—but it is fair to wonder how deleterious an effect the second operation will have on his often promising, ever frustrating career. We probably won't know the answer for a while. Taillon's operation occurred last August, meaning he might not reappear until the 2021 season. The way things are in baseball these days, let alone the world, it is hard to see anything beyond next season as guaranteed.

YEAR	TEAM	LVL	AGE	WHIP	ERA	DRA	WARP	MPH	FB%	WHF	CSP
2017	IND	AAA	25	1.27	4.09	3.59	0.3				
2017	PIT	MLB	25	1.48	4.44	4.08	2.2	97.1	64.1	9.6	48
2018	PIT	MLB	26	1.18	3.20	3.41	4.2	97.3	57.3	11.8	48.6
2019	PIT	MLB	27	1.12	4.10	3.74	0.8	96.9	47.2	12.5	48.3
2020	PIT	MLB	28	1.25	3.86	4.08	0.5	96.6	58.6	11.2	48.6

Jameson Taillon, continued

Pitch Shape vs LHH

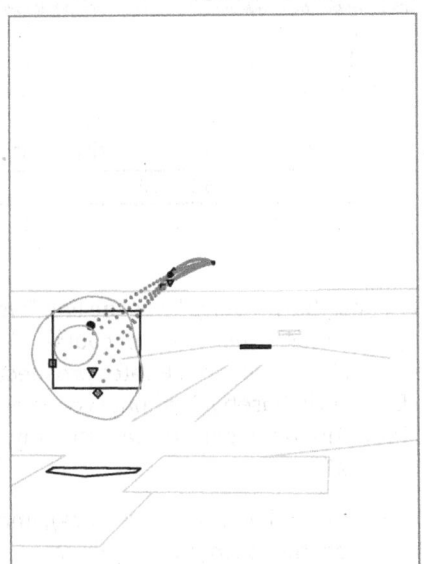

Pitch Shape vs RHH

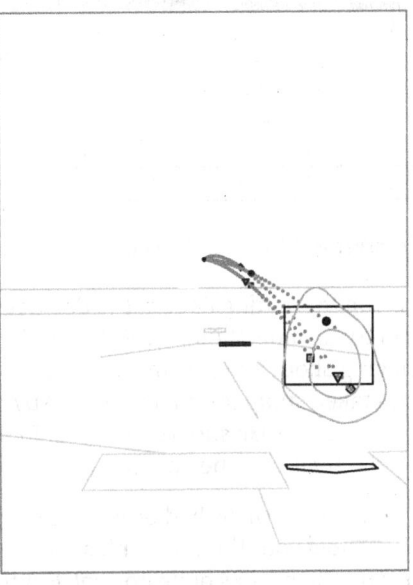

Type	Frequency	Velocity	H Movement	V Movement
● Fastball	27.1%	95.2 [108]	-0.8 [127]	-15.2 [102]
□ Sinker	20.1%	95.4 [115]	-10.1 [116]	-17.7 [109]
+ Cutter				
▲ Changeup	5.4%	88.5 [112]	-10.2 [105]	-24.7 [108]
✕ Splitter				
▽ Slider	31.6%	89.2 [120]	5 [100]	-26.1 [120]
◇ Curveball	15.7%	82.6 [113]	9.5 [108]	-46.2 [103]
⊕ Slow Curveball				
✳ Knuckleball				
▼ Screwball				

Wei-Chung Wang LHP

Born: 04/25/92   Age: 28   Bats: L   Throws: L
Height: 6'1"   Weight: 160   Origin: International Free Agent, 2011

YEAR	TEAM	LVL	AGE	W	L	SV	G	GS	IP	H	HR	BB/9	K/9	K	GB%	BABIP
2017	CSP	AAA	25	6	2	1	47	0	57	57	6	1.9	7.6	48	49%	.300
2017	MIL	MLB	25	0	0	0	8	0	1¹	5	1	0.0	13.5	2	43%	.667
2019	LVG	AAA	27	1	1	1	19	0	26¹	29	5	2.7	8.2	24	46%	.308
2019	OAK	MLB	27	1	0	0	20	0	27	22	4	3.7	5.3	16	30%	.231
2019	PIT	MLB	27	2	0	0	5	0	4	5	0	6.8	4.5	2	71%	.357
2020	PIT	MLB	28	2	2	0	33	0	35	37	7	3.3	6.6	26	40%	.280

Comparables: Tyler Wilson, Tyler Duffey, Brent Suter

Left on the cutting floor of the Bee Gees' 1977 hit "Stayin' Alive" was the line "we can try to understand/the Rule 5 draft's effect on man." They were, of course, singing about Wang, some 37 years before the then-21-year-old Pirates prospect was taken straight from rookie ball by the Brewers in baseball's annual version of a yard sale. He survived the year in the Show, thanks in part to a lengthy stay on the shelf, and then proceeded directly to A-ball.

Wang has always had promising stuff (hence Milwaukee's calculated risk), and if you hold your thumb over his weird 2014 season, his ascent up the minor-league chain looks quite normal. But the Brewers cut ties after 2017 and he found his way to a contract in Korea, possibly chasing the money, or the playing time, or bulgogi, or the chance to be closer to his native Taiwan.

The story could have easily ended there, with a pitcher going through a severe case of the transactional bends. However the Athletics tend to confound such narratives and did so here by giving him a chance to join their bullpen, where he was permitted his first sustained major league utility. He was even in a pennant race. The A's once again became the A's, shedding him once they needed a spot for A.J. Puk and concluding his ERA was on borrowed time. Off to the waiver wire Wang went, before completing the circuit by returning to the Pirates.

There are transactional wormholes everywhere and Wang has nearly rolled a Yahtzee on the gamut of them. But, sometimes, part of being a curious talent is staying alive through them before eventually finding the correct fit. For Wang's sake, here's hoping he's found it.

YEAR	TEAM	LVL	AGE	WHIP	ERA	DRA	WARP	MPH	FB%	WHF	CSP
2017	CSP	AAA	25	1.21	2.05	2.78	1.6				
2017	MIL	MLB	25	3.75	13.50	5.57	0.0	96.2	37.5	15.6	47.7
2019	LVG	AAA	27	1.41	4.78	3.74	0.6				
2019	OAK	MLB	27	1.22	3.33	7.42	-0.6	94.4	43.1	9.7	47.4
2019	PIT	MLB	27	2.00	6.75	1.94	0.1	94.0	47.4	5.1	41.4
2020	PIT	MLB	28	1.43	5.20	5.25	0.1	93.8	43.8	9.3	47.2

Pittsburgh Pirates 2020

Wei-Chung Wang, continued

Pitch Shape vs LHH

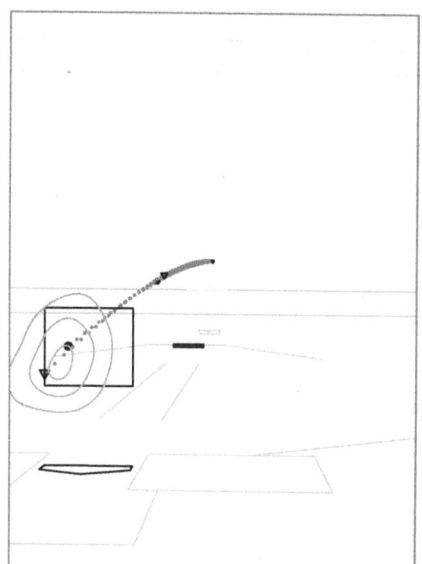

Pitch Shape vs RHH

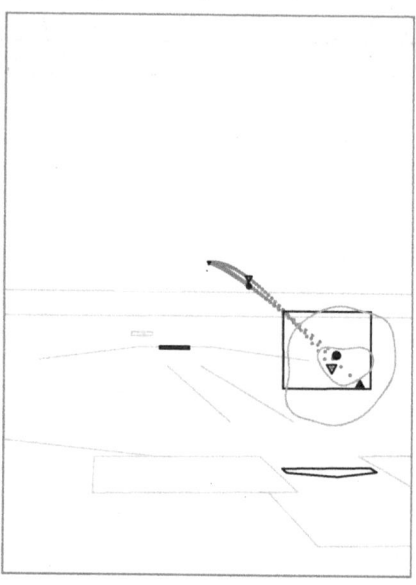

Type	Frequency	Velocity	H Movement	V Movement
● Fastball	43.4%	91.6 [98]	7.4 [97]	-14.2 [104]
☐ Sinker				
+ Cutter				
▲ Changeup	15.8%	83.9 [95]	11.8 [97]	-24.7 [108]
✕ Splitter				
▽ Slider	34.7%	84.7 [101]	-2.7 [90]	-28.7 [113]
◇ Curveball	5.8%	79.2 [102]	-3 [82]	-40.2 [116]
⊕ Slow Curveball				
✱ Knuckleball				
▼ Screwball				

Trevor Williams   RHP

Born: 04/25/92   Age: 28   Bats: R   Throws: R
Height: 6'3"   Weight: 230   Origin: Round 2, 2013 Draft (#44 overall)

YEAR	TEAM	LVL	AGE	W	L	SV	G	GS	IP	H	HR	BB/9	K/9	K	GB%	BABIP
2017	PIT	MLB	25	7	9	0	31	25	150^1	145	14	3.1	7.0	117	50%	.292
2018	PIT	MLB	26	14	10	0	31	31	170^2	146	15	2.9	6.6	126	43%	.261
2019	PIT	MLB	27	7	9	0	26	26	145^2	162	27	2.7	7.0	113	39%	.303
2020	PIT	MLB	28	9	10	0	28	28	154	157	24	2.9	7.0	121	40%	.289

Comparables: Jerad Eickhoff, Luis Cessa, Dillon Gee

An answer to a great trivia question no one will ever ask, Williams was acquired while he was a prospect as compensation for purported pitching guru Jim Benedict. (Benedict lasted all of two seasons in Miami.) His repertoire is low on frills—he hovers around the 20th percentile in fastball spin, curve spin and velocity—and he relies on contact management as opposed to missing bats. Williams used to be more of a ground-ball pitcher; in 2019, however, his batted-ball profile was tilted toward the air. In a sense, then, it's not too surprising that he had a shaky season the same year the ball was altered. Williams' stock was always going to be sensitive to external forces—that's the warp and the woof of the profile—and it'll be interesting to see what comes of his approach under the keen eye of new management.

YEAR	TEAM	LVL	AGE	WHIP	ERA	DRA	WARP	MPH	FB%	WHF	CSP
2017	PIT	MLB	25	1.31	4.07	4.49	1.8	95.0	71.6	9.1	46.4
2018	PIT	MLB	26	1.18	3.11	4.28	2.0	93.7	69.4	8.8	46
2019	PIT	MLB	27	1.41	5.38	5.74	0.1	93.9	66.7	11.2	46.2
2020	PIT	MLB	28	1.35	4.58	4.72	1.9	93.5	69.3	9.9	46.5

Pittsburgh Pirates 2020

Trevor Williams, continued

Pitch Shape vs LHH

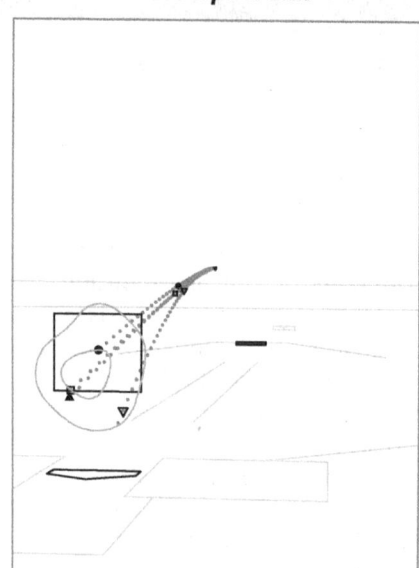

Pitch Shape vs RHH

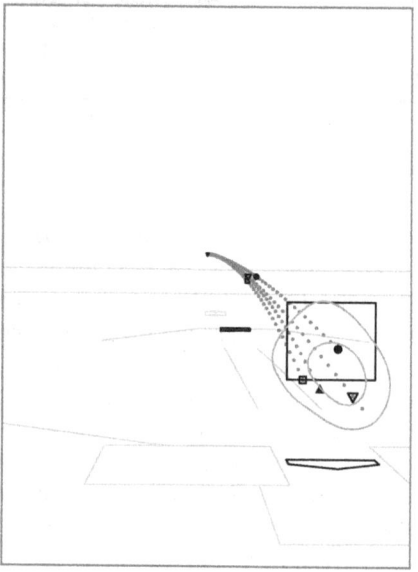

Type	Frequency	Velocity	H Movement	V Movement
● Fastball	52.0%	92.1 [99]	-5.4 [107]	-16.2 [99]
□ Sinker	14.7%	90 [87]	-12.5 [101]	-23.9 [88]
+ Cutter				
▲ Changeup	12.2%	84 [95]	-12.3 [95]	-26.5 [103]
× Splitter				
▽ Slider	20.1%	83.2 [95]	6 [104]	-33.4 [99]
◇ Curveball				
⊕ Slow Curveball				
✱ Knuckleball				
▼ Screwball				

PLAYER COMMENTS WITHOUT GRAPHS

Rodolfo Castro MI
Born: 05/21/99   Age: 21   Bats: B   Throws: R
Height: 6'0"   Weight: 200   Origin: International Free Agent, 2015

YEAR	TEAM	LVL	AGE	PA	R	2B	3B	HR	RBI	BB	K	SB	CS	AVG/OBP/SLG
2017	PIR	RK	18	211	27	12	4	6	32	16	47	4	3	.277/.344/.479
2018	WVA	A	19	426	47	19	4	12	50	26	100	6	3	.231/.278/.395
2019	GRB	A	20	246	33	13	2	14	46	18	68	6	5	.242/.306/.516
2019	BRD	A+	20	215	26	13	1	5	27	13	54	1	0	.243/.288/.391
2020	PIT	MLB	21	251	22	12	1	6	26	17	81	1	0	.206/.265/.351

Comparables: Dilson Herrera, Abiatal Avelino, Michael Chavis

Say this, Castro looks the part. Indeed, he looks the part so well that he appears to have been summoned from central casting when contrasted with the workmanlike collegiates and the stalled-out international signings that populate much of A-ball. He has smooth actions at the various infield positions, and enough arm to cover the demands of the left side. At the plate, his loose and whippy swing produces beautiful line drives all over. Unfortunately, looks aren't all that matters. Castro is prone to swinging and missing at breaking balls, a combination that could make him a well-below-average hitter. The rest of his tool box is heavy on 5's and light on anything else, so he might end up being no more than a bench type (albeit one with a convincing look).

YEAR	TEAM	LVL	AGE	PA	DRC+	VORP	BABIP	BRR	FRAA	WARP
2017	PIR	RK	18	211	120	18.1	.338	0.5	SS(19): 1.3, 3B(17): -4.4	0.9
2018	WVA	A	19	426	82	10.9	.276	2.9	2B(89): 4.3, SS(12): 1.6	1.4
2019	GRB	A	20	246	127	20.7	.271	2.1	2B(34): -0.2, SS(17): -0.9	1.6
2019	BRD	A+	20	215	105	8.0	.308	0.3	2B(36): 1.9, SS(16): -1.2	0.9
2020	PIT	MLB	21	251	63	-4.4	.285	-0.3	2B 1, SS 0	-0.4

Pittsburgh Pirates 2020

Will Craig 1B

Born: 11/16/94   Age: 25   Bats: R   Throws: R
Height: 6'3"   Weight: 212   Origin: Round 1, 2016 Draft (#22 overall)

YEAR	TEAM	LVL	AGE	PA	R	2B	3B	HR	RBI	BB	K	SB	CS	AVG/OBP/SLG
2017	BRD	A+	22	542	59	26	1	6	61	62	106	1	3	.271/.373/.371
2018	ALT	AA	23	549	73	30	3	20	102	42	128	6	3	.248/.321/.448
2019	IND	AAA	24	556	69	23	0	23	78	44	146	2	3	.249/.326/.435
2020	PIT	MLB	25	251	25	12	0	8	28	16	75	1	0	.223/.291/.381

Comparables: Travis Shaw, Christian Walker, Tyler Collins

Craig was a first-round pick in 2016 due to his offensive upside. He was never going to stick at third base, but the belief was that his strength, eye and feel for good contact would permit him to hit enough to survive a move across the diamond to first. Craig made the transition to the cold corner in 2018; his offensive acumen did not. Rather, he's walked less and struck out more in each of the past two seasons. He's remained a capable power threat, yet it's hard to see him being an above-average hitter in the majors when he can't be one in Triple-A. Maybe Craig turns the scooter around and becomes a Steve Pearce type; it seems more likely he's a Quad-A player.

YEAR	TEAM	LVL	AGE	PA	DRC+	VORP	BABIP	BRR	FRAA	WARP
2017	BRD	A+	22	542	144	11.7	.335	-7.8	1B(93): 9.4	2.9
2018	ALT	AA	23	549	111	28.6	.288	0.6	1B(122): 8.8	2.4
2019	IND	AAA	24	556	94	3.2	.304	-0.4	1B(110): 0.7, RF(13): -1.1	0.2
2020	PIT	MLB	25	251	78	0.4	.296	-0.5	1B 2, RF 0	0.3

Oneil Cruz SS

Born: 10/04/98   Age: 21   Bats: L   Throws: R
Height: 6'7"   Weight: 175   Origin: International Free Agent, 2015

YEAR	TEAM	LVL	AGE	PA	R	2B	3B	HR	RBI	BB	K	SB	CS	AVG/OBP/SLG
2017	GRL	A	18	375	51	9	1	8	36	28	110	8	7	.240/.293/.342
2017	WVA	A	18	63	9	2	1	2	8	8	22	0	0	.218/.317/.400
2018	WVA	A	19	443	66	25	7	14	59	34	100	11	5	.286/.343/.488
2019	BRD	A+	20	145	21	6	1	7	16	8	38	7	3	.301/.345/.515
2019	ALT	AA	20	136	14	8	3	1	17	15	35	3	1	.269/.346/.412
2020	PIT	MLB	21	251	24	12	1	7	27	18	80	3	1	.233/.290/.380

Comparables: Yorman Rodriguez, Alex Liddi, Andrew Velazquez

Let's start by addressing the unusually tall elephant in the room: Cruz is indeed a 6-foot-7 shortstop. Normally, that's an elaborate way of saying "a future third baseman." In Cruz's case, he can play the position thanks to his strong arm and high-grade athleticism. There is a good amount of variability with regards to his speed and power projections. He's an above-average runner for the time being, but that seems likely to change as he adds strength to his frame—a development that will better position him to tap into his raw power. As such, there's no telling exactly how Cruz will mature. He is, nonetheless, among the most intriguing prospects in the minors. Put a star next to his name, for if all goes well that's what he'll become.

YEAR	TEAM	LVL	AGE	PA	DRC+	VORP	BABIP	BRR	FRAA	WARP
2017	GRL	A	18	375	83	13.9	.323	3.2	3B(47): -9.3, SS(30): 0.2	-0.1
2017	WVA	A	18	63	78	3.4	.323	1.0	3B(15): 0.6, SS(1): 0.0	0.2
2018	WVA	A	19	443	130	37.7	.346	2.5	SS(102): -5.9	2.9
2019	BRD	A+	20	145	152	14.8	.374	0.1	SS(35): 2.2	1.6
2019	ALT	AA	20	136	121	10.1	.365	1.1	SS(34): 2.9	1.3
2020	PIT	MLB	21	251	77	0.6	.327	-0.2	SS 1, 3B 0	0.1

Matt Gorski CF

Born: 12/22/97 Age: 22 Bats: R Throws: R
Height: 6'4" Weight: 198 Origin: Round 2, 2019 Draft (#57 overall)

YEAR	TEAM	LVL	AGE	PA	R	2B	3B	HR	RBI	BB	K	SB	CS	AVG/OBP/SLG
2019	WEV	A-	21	202	32	9	2	3	22	19	48	11	3	.223/.297/.346
2020	PIT	MLB	22	251	20	11	1	4	22	15	80	2	1	.200/.250/.312

Comparables: Skye Bolt, Adam Haseley, Ryan Cordell

The surname Gorski has its roots in the Polish word for hill or mountain. Shamelessly, we must note that Gorski's path to Pittsburgh will be steep. His swing can get long and results in whiffs by the truck haul—hence his 24 percent K rate in his initial exposure to pro ball. Gorski does have a nice combination of power and athleticism going for him, but he's more of a project than you'd suspect for a collegiate second-round pick.

YEAR	TEAM	LVL	AGE	PA	DRC+	VORP	BABIP	BRR	FRAA	WARP
2019	WEV	A-	21	202	85	6.5	.282	2.2	CF(21): 0.2, LF(19): 2.9	0.8
2020	PIT	MLB	22	251	50	-8.2	.282	0.0	CF 1, LF 1	-0.6

Ke'Bryan Hayes 3B

Born: 01/28/97 Age: 23 Bats: R Throws: R
Height: 6'1" Weight: 210 Origin: Round 1, 2015 Draft (#32 overall)

YEAR	TEAM	LVL	AGE	PA	R	2B	3B	HR	RBI	BB	K	SB	CS	AVG/OBP/SLG
2017	BRD	A+	20	482	66	16	7	2	43	41	76	27	5	.278/.345/.363
2018	ALT	AA	21	508	64	31	7	7	47	57	84	12	5	.293/.375/.444
2019	IND	AAA	22	480	64	30	2	10	53	43	90	12	1	.265/.336/.415
2020	PIT	MLB	23	42	4	2	0	1	4	3	10	1	0	.231/.298/.356

Comparables: Jefry Marte, Miguel Andújar, Rio Ruiz

Charlie's kid continued his methodical climb through the minors in 2019, as he spent the season at Triple-A. It's a little concerning that Hayes required the altered ball to reach double-digit home runs for the first time in his career, and it's a lot concerning that he graded as a below-average hitter overall. The optimistic projection here is the same—that he'll be an asset on both sides of the ball. But Hayes turned 23 in January and it's (still) fair to question if his bat is going to hold up its part of the bargain.

YEAR	TEAM	LVL	AGE	PA	DRC+	VORP	BABIP	BRR	FRAA	WARP
2017	BRD	A+	20	482	124	18.8	.331	0.8	3B(108): 20.7	4.9
2018	ALT	AA	21	508	133	38.7	.344	-0.8	3B(116): 9.0	4.5
2019	IND	AAA	22	480	96	14.6	.311	2.3	3B(103): 8.2	2.3
2020	PIT	MLB	23	42	74	-0.4	.290	0.0	3B 1	0.0

Pittsburgh Pirates 2020

Kevin Kramer 2B

Born: 10/03/93 Age: 26 Bats: L Throws: R
Height: 6'0" Weight: 200 Origin: Round 2, 2015 Draft (#62 overall)

YEAR	TEAM	LVL	AGE	PA	R	2B	3B	HR	RBI	BB	K	SB	CS	AVG/OBP/SLG
2017	ALT	AA	23	234	31	17	3	6	27	17	50	7	2	.297/.380/.500
2018	IND	AAA	24	527	73	35	3	15	59	38	127	13	5	.311/.365/.492
2018	PIT	MLB	24	40	5	0	0	0	4	2	20	0	0	.135/.175/.135
2019	IND	AAA	25	448	49	30	1	10	54	43	116	4	5	.260/.335/.417
2019	PIT	MLB	25	50	5	1	0	0	5	6	17	0	1	.167/.260/.190
2020	PIT	MLB	26	105	10	5	0	2	10	8	31	1	1	.218/.284/.348

Comparables: Preston Tucker, Nick Solak, Ryan Adams

For a second consecutive season Kramer received a 20-something-game look, and for a second consecutive season Kramer failed to make his mark. In theory, he should be able to land on a bench thanks to a decent bat and the ability to stand on the dirt or grass alike; in practice, that hasn't been the case, leaving him another rough circle around the sun from hitting the waiver wire. The good news for Kramer—and for anyone who loves making easy *Seinfeld* jokes—is that there's a general manager named Jerry who would likely give him a spot if it comes to that.

YEAR	TEAM	LVL	AGE	PA	DRC+	VORP	BABIP	BRR	FRAA	WARP
2017	ALT	AA	23	234	124	20.8	.362	1.7	2B(48): -1.6	1.3
2018	IND	AAA	24	527	146	42.2	.392	1.7	2B(82): -6.3, 3B(19): 0.9	3.7
2018	PIT	MLB	24	40	56	-3.3	.278	0.5	3B(7): -0.3, 2B(4): -0.6	-0.1
2019	IND	AAA	25	448	102	11.9	.336	-2.2	2B(50): 1.2, LF(20): 0.6	1.0
2019	PIT	MLB	25	50	66	-0.9	.259	0.7	RF(7): 0.0, LF(7): -0.9	-0.1
2020	PIT	MLB	26	105	68	-1.5	.296	-0.2	2B 0, LF -1	-0.3

Jason Martin CF

Born: 09/05/95 Age: 24 Bats: L Throws: R
Height: 5'9" Weight: 185 Origin: Round 8, 2013 Draft (#227 overall)

YEAR	TEAM	LVL	AGE	PA	R	2B	3B	HR	RBI	BB	K	SB	CS	AVG/OBP/SLG
2017	BCA	A+	21	198	34	11	2	7	29	20	42	9	5	.287/.354/.494
2017	CCH	AA	21	320	38	24	3	11	37	19	82	7	6	.273/.319/.483
2018	ALT	AA	22	289	49	13	5	9	34	28	61	7	8	.325/.392/.522
2018	IND	AAA	22	234	20	5	3	4	21	17	52	5	4	.211/.270/.319
2019	IND	AAA	23	406	47	25	5	8	50	29	79	9	6	.259/.312/.419
2019	PIT	MLB	23	40	5	2	0	0	2	4	10	2	0	.250/.325/.306
2020	PIT	MLB	24	147	14	7	1	4	16	10	37	3	2	.223/.275/.378

Comparables: Dalton Pompey, Dick Williams, Willy García

The forgotten part of the Gerrit Cole trade, Martin actually attended the same high school as Cole—Orange Lutheran, in California. That's where the similarities end between the two. Martin is one of several outfielders in the system with a few decent characteristics: athleticism, speed, hit tool and glove (albeit just in a corner). He debuted in the majors last season and required shoulder surgery late in the year to repair a labral tear. Martin should get more big-league burn this season, but there's no reason to expect him to become more than a reserve type, if that.

YEAR	TEAM	LVL	AGE	PA	DRC+	VORP	BABIP	BRR	FRAA	WARP
2017	BCA	A+	21	198	142	13.1	.333	-1.6	LF(25): 1.1, CF(12): -2.2	1.0
2017	CCH	AA	21	320	122	15.2	.343	1.1	LF(57): -6.9	0.7
2018	ALT	AA	22	289	143	31.7	.396	-0.7	CF(62): -2.4, LF(6): -0.6	1.9
2018	IND	AAA	22	234	63	-5.5	.261	-0.6	CF(53): -6.5, LF(6): -0.3	-0.8
2019	IND	AAA	23	406	90	6.7	.307	0.8	CF(92): -4.1, LF(4): -0.7	0.5
2019	PIT	MLB	23	40	73	-0.2	.346	0.5	LF(12): -0.6, CF(3): 0.1	0.0
2020	PIT	MLB	24	147	69	-1.6	.275	-0.1	LF 0, CF 0	-0.2

Mason Martin 1B

Born: 06/02/99 Age: 21 Bats: L Throws: R
Height: 6'0" Weight: 201 Origin: Round 17, 2017 Draft (#508 overall)

YEAR	TEAM	LVL	AGE	PA	R	2B	3B	HR	RBI	BB	K	SB	CS	AVG/OBP/SLG
2017	PIR	RK	18	166	37	8	0	11	22	32	41	2	2	.307/.457/.630
2018	BRI	RK	19	269	42	10	1	10	40	42	87	2	2	.233/.357/.422
2018	WVA	A	19	173	16	8	0	4	18	18	62	1	1	.200/.302/.333
2019	GRB	A	20	355	58	19	3	23	83	46	103	8	2	.262/.361/.575
2019	BRD	A+	20	201	32	13	1	12	46	22	65	0	1	.239/.333/.528
2020	PIT	MLB	21	251	24	12	1	7	26	26	93	0	0	.189/.281/.339

Comparables: Tyler O'Neill, Matt Olson, Travis Demeritte

Yes, the Pirates have a Jason Martin *and* a Mason Martin. The wonders of the universe, y'all. This Martin is more interesting—provided you're into first-only prospects decimating the low-minors. He isn't going to wow you with athleticism in the field—obviously, he's a young first baseman—or even at the plate, but he has an excellent approach, adjusts well and does a nice job waiting for a pitch he can drive. Martin is far, far from a high-upside play, yet he's been effective so far in his young career and left-handed pop is always nice to have. Now, whom do we have to talk to about the Pirates landing a Cason Martin?

YEAR	TEAM	LVL	AGE	PA	DRC+	VORP	BABIP	BRR	FRAA	WARP
2017	PIR	RK	18	166	216	23.3	.368	-2.2	1B(26): 1.5, RF(9): -1.2	1.5
2018	BRI	RK	19	269	109	8.1	.328	1.4	1B(52): -1.7	0.5
2018	WVA	A	19	173	80	0.8	.310	0.0	1B(43): -3.0	-0.5
2019	GRB	A	20	355	163	33.3	.311	-1.5	1B(77): 4.1	2.9
2019	BRD	A+	20	201	130	8.8	.303	-0.8	1B(46): 3.4	1.1
2020	PIT	MLB	21	251	67	-3.0	.287	-0.3	1B 2, RF 0	-0.1

Cal Mitchell RF

Born: 03/08/99   Age: 21   Bats: L   Throws: L
Height: 6'0"   Weight: 209   Origin: Round 2, 2017 Draft (#50 overall)

YEAR	TEAM	LVL	AGE	PA	R	2B	3B	HR	RBI	BB	K	SB	CS	AVG/OBP/SLG
2017	PIR	RK	18	185	17	11	0	2	20	24	35	2	3	.245/.351/.352
2018	WVA	A	19	495	55	29	3	10	65	41	109	4	5	.280/.344/.427
2019	BRD	A+	20	493	54	21	2	15	64	32	142	1	1	.251/.304/.406
2020	PIT	MLB	21	251	25	12	1	7	28	20	81	0	0	.234/.299/.389

Comparables: Dalton Pompey, Willy García, Yorman Rodriguez

If there's one thing the Pirates have done well in recent years it's produce somewhat competent, ultimately underwhelming position players. Mitchell could be the next in line—and hey, they do have value—provided he finds some balance in his game, but it's no sure thing. Mitchell is known primarily for a sweet swing (they always look nicer from the left side) and some hitting promise for a reason—that reason being he doesn't offer much secondary value. Mitchell doesn't offer heapings of primary value, either. His strikeout rate could bloat into the 30-percent range in Double-A, and he's unlikely to walk and bop enough to make up for it. We'll see how his age-21 season goes, but we'd feel better about Mitchell's overcoming the deficiencies in his profile if the strengths were stronger.

YEAR	TEAM	LVL	AGE	PA	DRC+	VORP	BABIP	BRR	FRAA	WARP
2017	PIR	RK	18	185	123	4.8	.303	-0.9	LF(35): 2.6, CF(3): 0.5	0.9
2018	WVA	A	19	495	127	20.4	.347	-4.4	RF(100): 0.5, LF(11): -1.6	1.7
2019	BRD	A+	20	493	104	8.5	.328	0.0	RF(110): -0.4	1.0
2020	PIT	MLB	21	251	82	1.8	.328	-0.4	RF 0, LF 0	0.2

Pittsburgh Pirates 2020

Jared Oliva CF

Born: 11/27/95   Age: 24   Bats: R   Throws: R
Height: 6'3"   Weight: 203   Origin: Round 7, 2017 Draft (#208 overall)

YEAR	TEAM	LVL	AGE	PA	R	2B	3B	HR	RBI	BB	K	SB	CS	AVG/OBP/SLG
2017	WEV	A-	21	254	30	10	7	0	17	17	57	15	4	.266/.327/.374
2018	BRD	A+	22	454	75	24	4	9	47	40	91	33	8	.275/.354/.424
2019	ALT	AA	23	507	70	24	6	6	42	42	104	36	10	.277/.352/.398
2020	PIT	MLB	24	251	24	12	2	5	24	16	67	9	3	.236/.298/.362

Comparables: Bryan Reynolds, Jake Marisnick, Tyler Naquin

Oliva is an average all-around player, which, if you think about it, translates to above-average in the general scheme of things. He's a pretty good runner, a pretty good defender in center with a pretty good arm, and he can hit a little more than a little. Not too shabby for a seventh rounder who could well bring his game to the Steel City before 2020 ends.

YEAR	TEAM	LVL	AGE	PA	DRC+	VORP	BABIP	BRR	FRAA	WARP
2017	WEV	A-	21	254	97	9.3	.353	-0.4	CF(42): 0.6, LF(6): -0.2	0.7
2018	BRD	A+	22	454	129	28.7	.332	4.3	CF(101): -7.6	2.4
2019	ALT	AA	23	507	128	34.4	.347	4.2	CF(113): -1.2, LF(1): -0.1	3.4
2020	PIT	MLB	24	251	76	1.4	.314	1.0	CF 0, LF 0	0.1

Liover Peguero SS

Born: 12/31/00 Age: 19 Bats: R Throws: R
Height: 6'1" Weight: 160 Origin: International Free Agent, 2017

YEAR	TEAM	LVL	AGE	PA	R	2B	3B	HR	RBI	BB	K	SB	CS	AVG/OBP/SLG
2018	DDI	RK	17	90	14	3	3	1	16	6	12	4	1	.309/.356/.457
2018	DIA	RK	17	71	8	0	0	0	5	5	17	3	2	.197/.254/.197
2019	MSO	RK+	18	156	34	7	3	5	27	12	34	8	1	.364/.410/.559
2019	YAK	A-	18	93	13	4	2	0	11	8	17	3	1	.262/.333/.357
2020	ARI	MLB	19	251	21	11	2	3	23	16	71	3	1	.239/.291/.343

Comparables: Amed Rosario, Enrique Hernández, Willi Castro

The Diamondbacks are chock full of toolsy, young shortstop prospects and Peguero is the newest of the bunch, but might have as much upside as any of them. He's got a good shot to stick at the six, and he projects to have potential plus power that he can get to in games. Geraldo Perdomo gets most of the attention when it comes to up-and-coming shortstop prospects in the Arizona system, but don't sleep on Peguero, whose advanced barrel control and explosive bat speed give him a lofty ceiling.

YEAR	TEAM	LVL	AGE	PA	DRC+	VORP	BABIP	BRR	FRAA	WARP
2018	DDI	RK	17	90	128	8.4	.343	-0.3	SS(21): 0.9	0.7
2018	DIA	RK	17	71	76	-4.5	.265	-0.9	SS(19): 2.2	0.3
2019	MSO	RK+	18	156	154	22.1	.448	1.7		1.6
2019	YAK	A-	18	93	104	3.5	.328	0.1	SS(18): -0.1	0.4
2020	ARI	MLB	19	251	70	-1.8	.328	0.0	SS 1	0.0

Lolo Sanchez OF

Born: 04/23/99 Age: 21 Bats: R Throws: R
Height: 5'11" Weight: 168 Origin: International Free Agent, 2015

YEAR	TEAM	LVL	AGE	PA	R	2B	3B	HR	RBI	BB	K	SB	CS	AVG/OBP/SLG
2017	PIR	RK	18	234	42	11	2	4	20	21	19	14	7	.284/.359/.417
2018	WVA	A	19	441	57	18	1	4	34	41	72	30	13	.243/.322/.328
2019	GRB	A	20	263	43	10	6	4	26	17	28	20	10	.301/.377/.451
2019	BRD	A+	20	195	21	3	3	1	9	18	31	13	5	.196/.300/.270
2020	PIT	MLB	21	251	21	11	1	3	21	18	46	7	4	.217/.287/.314

Comparables: Abiatal Avelino, Abraham Almonte, Jason Martin

Sanchez is the kind of player that reminds you baseball is in the entertainment business. Daddy Yankee circa 2005 bumping as he settles into the box, a ball sliced down the third-base line, 12ish seconds and a slide into third. The A-ball crowd roars, probably the first and only time tonight everyone's eyes are fixed on the field. Did we mention he plays an excellent center field? All right, now that we've gotten you excited, we would be remiss if we didn't let you in on a few things; after all, if things were as rosy as portrayed over the first few sentences, you wouldn't be staring at a stat-line featuring an OPS under .600 post-promotion to Advanced-A. He has a quick bat but a questionable bat path—put another way, he is built like Rajai Davis but swings like Pete Alonso, which leads to more soft contact in the air than you'd like from the speedy dude bookending your lineup. He's had just one combined above-average offensive season in his pro career as a result, yet he's still young and armed with impressive tools and a great taste in music—that counts for something in this book.

YEAR	TEAM	LVL	AGE	PA	DRC+	VORP	BABIP	BRR	FRAA	WARP
2017	PIR	RK	18	234	126	14.9	.295	-0.9	CF(49): 7.6	1.9
2018	WVA	A	19	441	97	14.2	.287	2.7	CF(88): 8.4, LF(19): -2.1	2.1
2019	GRB	A	20	263	142	25.5	.327	2.1	CF(40): -3.7, LF(14): 0.5	1.8
2019	BRD	A+	20	195	63	1.1	.233	2.4	LF(41): 0.3, CF(4): -0.8	-0.1
2020	PIT	MLB	21	251	63	-4.1	.260	0.0	CF 1, LF -1	-0.3

Sammy Siani CF

Born: 12/14/00 Age: 19 Bats: L Throws: L
Height: 6'0" Weight: 195 Origin: Round 1, 2019 Draft (#37 overall)

YEAR	TEAM	LVL	AGE	PA	R	2B	3B	HR	RBI	BB	K	SB	CS	AVG/OBP/SLG
2019	PIR	RK	18	164	21	3	3	0	9	26	41	5	0	.241/.372/.308
2020	PIT	MLB	19	251	21	11	1	3	20	23	85	3	1	.209/.287/.302

Comparables: Derrick Robinson, Brett Phillips, Jason Martin

An overslot CBA selection from the other side of Pennsylvania, Sammy became the second Siani to forgo an ACC commitment to play pro ball: he skipped Duke after his brother Mike spurned Virginia to sign with Cincinnati. He isn't as overloaded with upside as some prep guys, but as a sweet-swinging lefty-hitting corner outfielder he shares some similarities with Mitchell.

YEAR	TEAM	LVL	AGE	PA	DRC+	VORP	BABIP	BRR	FRAA	WARP
2019	PIR	RK	18	164	95	2.5	.340	-1.1	CF(21): -3.0, LF(16): 1.4	0.1
2020	PIT	MLB	19	251	62	-4.2	.322	0.0	CF -1, LF 0	-0.5

Pittsburgh Pirates 2020

Travis Swaggerty CF
Born: 08/19/97   Age: 22   Bats: L   Throws: L
Height: 5'11"   Weight: 180   Origin: Round 1, 2018 Draft (#10 overall)

YEAR	TEAM	LVL	AGE	PA	R	2B	3B	HR	RBI	BB	K	SB	CS	AVG/OBP/SLG
2018	WEV	A-	20	158	22	9	1	4	15	15	40	9	3	.288/.365/.453
2018	WVA	A	20	71	6	1	1	1	5	7	18	0	0	.129/.225/.226
2019	BRD	A+	21	524	79	20	3	9	40	57	116	23	8	.265/.347/.381
2020	PIT	MLB	22	251	23	11	1	5	25	17	74	3	1	.223/.280/.347

Comparables: Daniel Fields, Zoilo Almonte, Kirk Nieuwenhuis

Swaggerty may seem familiar—not only because his name sounds like that of a character from *Deadwood*, but also because he's a former No. 10 pick who was the subject of a lot of chatter as he gained draft helium. Not hailing from South Dakota (rather South Alabama), Swaggerty is armed with a full set of tools. They're more fives and sixes than anything double-plus, but the overall package should be at least an above-average centerfielder in his early years plying power and speed as his trade.

YEAR	TEAM	LVL	AGE	PA	DRC+	VORP	BABIP	BRR	FRAA	WARP
2018	WEV	A-	20	158	151	12.5	.379	0.9	CF(36): -0.6	1.2
2018	WVA	A	20	71	40	-1.2	.159	-0.6	CF(16): 0.7	-0.2
2019	BRD	A+	21	524	124	25.2	.334	-0.2	CF(120): 7.4	3.7
2020	PIT	MLB	22	251	67	-2.6	.302	0.2	CF 2	-0.1

Braxton Ashcraft RHP

Born: 10/05/99 Age: 20 Bats: L Throws: R
Height: 6'5" Weight: 195 Origin: Round 2, 2018 Draft (#51 overall)

YEAR	TEAM	LVL	AGE	W	L	SV	G	GS	IP	H	HR	BB/9	K/9	K	GB%	BABIP
2018	PIR	RK	18	0	1	0	5	5	17²	16	2	2.5	6.1	12	52%	.259
2019	WEV	A-	19	1	9	0	11	11	53	49	4	3.7	6.6	39	45%	.273
2020	PIT	MLB	20	2	2	0	33	0	35	35	6	3.6	5.1	20	40%	.266

Comparables: Alex Cobb, Jake Brigham, Peter Lambert

Ashcraft is a tall, projectable, former two-sport athlete from Texas who pairs a mid-90s fastball with some in-progress secondaries. You probably guessed he was a second-round pick just from reading that description. (He was.) There's a long time between now and when (if) Ashcraft debuts, so we'll save our jokes about how he'll one day be traded for Tyler Glasnow for 2021.

YEAR	TEAM	LVL	AGE	WHIP	ERA	DRA	WARP	MPH	FB%	WHF	CSP
2018	PIR	RK	18	1.19	4.58	3.27	0.5				
2019	WEV	A-	19	1.34	5.77	5.18	0.0				
2020	PIT	MLB	20	1.40	4.80	4.95	0.2				

Osvaldo Bido RHP

Born: 10/18/95 Age: 24 Bats: R Throws: R
Height: 6'3" Weight: 175 Origin: International Free Agent, 2017

YEAR	TEAM	LVL	AGE	W	L	SV	G	GS	IP	H	HR	BB/9	K/9	K	GB%	BABIP
2017	DPI	RK	21	1	8	0	15	13	50²	53	1	6.4	7.3	41	57%	.333
2018	WEV	A-	22	4	6	0	14	14	75¹	74	2	2.3	6.9	58	62%	.320
2019	GRB	A	23	11	5	0	20	20	111²	94	9	2.3	7.3	90	42%	.267
2019	BRD	A+	23	1	3	0	5	5	24	18	1	3.4	6.4	17	42%	.243
2020	PIT	MLB	24	2	2	0	33	0	35	34	5	3.3	5.7	22	44%	.268

Comparables: Tyson Brummett, James Marvel, Daniel Ponce de Leon

The long and lanky Bido has a pleasing ratio of vowels to syllables in his name. He also had a pleasing stretch of performance in his age-23 season. He's a somewhat late developer, having just been promoted to High-A to finish the season, but his stuff makes him a name worth watching. Bido touches the mid-90s with his heater and commands it well enough as well. His slider isn't quite there, and so if he's going to reach the majors it's likely to be as an arm-strength reliever.

YEAR	TEAM	LVL	AGE	WHIP	ERA	DRA	WARP	MPH	FB%	WHF	CSP
2017	DPI	RK	21	1.76	5.33	7.15	-0.6				
2018	WEV	A-	22	1.23	4.18	5.17	0.0				
2019	GRB	A	23	1.10	3.55	4.54	0.8				
2019	BRD	A+	23	1.12	2.25	4.16	0.3				
2020	PIT	MLB	24	1.33	4.31	4.54	0.3				

Cody Bolton RHP

Born: 06/19/98 Age: 22 Bats: R Throws: R
Height: 6'3" Weight: 185 Origin: Round 6, 2017 Draft (#178 overall)

YEAR	TEAM	LVL	AGE	W	L	SV	G	GS	IP	H	HR	BB/9	K/9	K	GB%	BABIP
2017	PIR	RK	19	0	2	0	9	9	25^2	23	1	2.8	7.7	22	44%	.286
2018	WVA	A	20	3	3	0	9	9	44^1	43	6	1.4	9.1	45	43%	.308
2019	BRD	A+	21	6	3	0	12	12	61^2	39	1	2.0	10.1	69	48%	.245
2019	ALT	AA	21	2	3	0	9	9	40	37	6	3.6	7.4	33	35%	.277
2020	PIT	MLB	22	2	2	0	33	0	35	35	6	3.8	8.1	32	37%	.296

Comparables: Tyler Mahle, Edwin Díaz, Kyle Drabek

Bolton, a former sixth-round pick, has a lively fastball down in the zone and an advanced command profile—the combination of which made him lights out in the Florida State League. He scuffled a bit upon his promotion to Double-A, but it's important to remember that he won't turn 22 until next June. The more concerning matter is why he goes by "Cody" when his legal name is "Carl Donovan Bolton."

YEAR	TEAM	LVL	AGE	WHIP	ERA	DRA	WARP	MPH	FB%	WHF	CSP
2017	PIR	RK	19	1.21	3.16	2.84	0.9				
2018	WVA	A	20	1.13	3.65	4.28	0.5				
2019	BRD	A+	21	0.86	1.61	2.73	1.7				
2019	ALT	AA	21	1.33	5.85	4.31	0.3				
2020	PIT	MLB	22	1.43	4.78	4.89	0.2				

Santiago Florez RHP
Born: 05/09/00 Age: 20 Bats: R Throws: R
Height: 6'5" Weight: 222 Origin: International Free Agent, 2016

YEAR	TEAM	LVL	AGE	W	L	SV	G	GS	IP	H	HR	BB/9	K/9	K	GB%	BABIP
2017	DPI	RK	17	2	5	0	14	14	53^1	43	2	6.4	5.1	30	46%	.243
2018	PIR	RK	18	5	2	0	10	10	43^1	37	0	4.8	7.3	35	55%	.289
2019	BRI	RK+	19	2	2	0	10	10	41^2	35	4	4.5	7.8	36	49%	.267
2020									No projection							

Originally a low-money signing out of Colombia, Florez had himself a nice year. The opposition must experience some sensory overload when facing him due to his size and stuff—he has mid-90s heat and a promising curveball. Florez is years away from being years away, but if the Pirates are going to be praised for their international scouting prowess anytime soon, he figures to play a role.

YEAR	TEAM	LVL	AGE	WHIP	ERA	DRA	WARP	MPH	FB%	WHF	CSP
2017	DPI	RK	17	1.52	4.56	4.87	0.7				
2018	PIR	RK	18	1.38	4.15	5.09	0.5				
2019	BRI	RK+	19	1.34	3.46	4.20	0.9				
2020						No projection					

Steven Jennings RHP

Born: 11/13/98 Age: 21 Bats: R Throws: R
Height: 6'2" Weight: 175 Origin: Round 2, 2017 Draft (#42 overall)

YEAR	TEAM	LVL	AGE	W	L	SV	G	GS	IP	H	HR	BB/9	K/9	K	GB%	BABIP
2017	PIR	RK	18	0	2	0	10	10	26^1	31	2	3.4	4.4	13	57%	.305
2018	BRI	RK	19	3	4	0	13	13	65^1	68	5	3.7	7.3	53	46%	.307
2019	GRB	A	20	7	12	0	27	27	130	134	15	2.7	8.0	115	37%	.316
2020	PIT	MLB	21	2	2	0	33	0	35	36	6	3.9	6.2	24	34%	.278

Comparables: Yennsy Diaz, Elvin Ramirez, Anthony Banda

A second-round pick three years ago out of a Tennessee high school, Jennings is a command pitcher who lacks command. His problem isn't with control—or, the ability most closely linked to walks—but with leaving too many of his pitches center-cut. That's a teensy weensy problem given he lacks the overpowering stuff required to cover up for his location-based deficiencies. Jennings is still young and athletic enough to envision growth on this front. But, as our friend Brendon Urie is prone to saying, it's best to face these kinds of things with a sense of poise and rationality. That's why we're concluding that Jennings probably won't make the gains he needs to become a mid-rotation starter like the Pirates' original projection.

YEAR	TEAM	LVL	AGE	WHIP	ERA	DRA	WARP	MPH	FB%	WHF	CSP
2017	PIR	RK	18	1.56	4.10	5.98	0.0				
2018	BRI	RK	19	1.45	4.82	4.64	1.0				
2019	GRB	A	20	1.33	4.71	5.89	-1.1				
2020	PIT	MLB	21	1.47	5.13	5.17	0.1				

Pittsburgh Pirates 2020

Chad Kuhl RHP
Born: 09/10/92   Age: 27   Bats: R   Throws: R
Height: 6'3"   Weight: 216   Origin: Round 9, 2013 Draft (#269 overall)

YEAR	TEAM	LVL	AGE	W	L	SV	G	GS	IP	H	HR	BB/9	K/9	K	GB%	BABIP
2017	PIT	MLB	24	8	11	0	31	31	157^1	159	17	4.1	8.1	142	43%	.321
2018	PIT	MLB	25	5	5	0	16	16	85	89	14	3.5	8.6	81	41%	.311
2020	PIT	MLB	27	6	8	0	50	16	117	125	21	3.4	8.8	114	42%	.314

Comparables: Reynaldo López, Robert Gsellman, Sal Romano

Kuhl spent the year mending elbow scars and watching the world burn in front of him in the form of the self-immolations of the Pirates roster and front office. As hard as it is for a pitcher to sit out a season, he should be ready to partake in the latest New Era of Pirates Baseball come spring—and he'll do so without having that 2019 funk on him. Provided Kuhl can come back with his pitch gang intact—we're talking his mid-90s sinker and pair of breakers—then he has a chance to bring some peace to the universe, or, at least, the back of the rotation.

YEAR	TEAM	LVL	AGE	WHIP	ERA	DRA	WARP	MPH	FB%	WHF	CSP
2017	PIT	MLB	24	1.47	4.35	5.35	0.4	98.2	63.5	10.3	47.7
2018	PIT	MLB	25	1.44	4.55	4.24	1.0	97.8	59	10.3	49.3
2020	PIT	MLB	27	1.45	5.21	5.19	0.7	97.5	62.4	10.5	49.2

Quinn Priester RHP

Born: 09/15/00 Age: 19 Bats: R Throws: R
Height: 6'3" Weight: 195 Origin: Round 1, 2019 Draft (#18 overall)

YEAR	TEAM	LVL	AGE	W	L	SV	G	GS	IP	H	HR	BB/9	K/9	K	GB%	BABIP
2019	PIR	RK	18	1	1	0	8	7	32²	29	1	2.8	10.2	37	58%	.318
2020	PIT	MLB	19	2	2	0	33	0	35	35	5	3.8	7.7	30	48%	.289

Comparables: Domingo Germán, Sandy Baez, Alex Reyes

It may seem that your favorite team's chances of developing a front-end starter are the same an Umberto Eco character has at tracking down an apocryphal Christian king. Pirates fans know what we're talking about—Lord, do they—but they'll still dream on Priester, a first-round prep righty from the Chicago area who has two or three potential plus pitches in his fastballs (a four- and a two-seam version) and his curve. Priester was born on September 15, 2000. On that same day, the Pirates dropped a game to the Brewers. The losing pitcher was Matt Skrmetta, who feels as unreal as Prester John. We mention that to show quickly time moves, and how soon another failure to develop an ace could become just another minute in a sad fan's hour.

YEAR	TEAM	LVL	AGE	WHIP	ERA	DRA	WARP	MPH	FB%	WHF	CSP
2019	PIR	RK	18	1.19	3.03	5.66	0.1				
2020	PIT	MLB	19	1.42	4.78	4.91	0.2				

Tahnaj Thomas   RHP

Born: 06/16/99   Age: 21   Bats: R   Throws: R
Height: 6'4"   Weight: 190   Origin: International Free Agent, 2016

YEAR	TEAM	LVL	AGE	W	L	SV	G	GS	IP	H	HR	BB/9	K/9	K	GB%	BABIP
2017	CLE	RK	18	0	3	0	13	10	33	35	4	6.8	7.9	29	48%	.330
2018	CLE	RK	19	0	0	0	8	6	19^2	13	2	4.6	12.4	27	60%	.275
2019	BRI	RK+	20	2	3	0	12	12	48^1	40	5	2.6	11.0	59	42%	.292
2020								No projection								

Writing that the Bahamas have become a destination for scouts feels like a cheeky quip, but it's true—and it's true in part because of pitchers like Thomas. Acquired from Cleveland in the blockbuster trade that saw Jordan Luplow and Erik González swap sides, Thomas is a good athlete with an excellent frame and some projection. He has a mid-90s heater and a touch for his breaking stuff. It's true his command isn't up to snuff; it's true he hasn't pitched above rookie ball; and it's, uh, also true that nitpicking 20-year-olds with this much potential is akin to complaining about an afternoon in the Bahamas because a cloud blocked out the sun for a few minutes.

YEAR	TEAM	LVL	AGE	WHIP	ERA	DRA	WARP	MPH	FB%	WHF	CSP
2017	CLE	RK	18	1.82	6.00	7.41	-0.5				
2018	CLE	RK	19	1.17	4.58	2.13	0.8				
2019	BRI	RK+	20	1.12	3.17	3.77	1.3				
2020						No projection					

LINEOUTS

Hitters

HITTER	POS	TEAM	LVL	AGE	PA	R	2B	3B	HR	RBI	BB	K	SB	CS	AVG/OBP/SLG	DRC+	WARP
Ji-Hwan Bae	MI	GRB	A	19	380	69	25	5	0	38	43	77	31	11	.323/.403/.430	158	3.8
Steven Baron	C	PIT	MLB	28	10	0	1	0	0	1	0	6	0	0	.200/.200/.300	67	0.0
	C	IND	AAA	28	149	17	3	0	2	8	13	38	0	0	.180/.264/.248	46	-0.3
Socrates Brito	OF	TOR	MLB	26	43	5	0	1	0	2	4	17	0	0	.077/.163/.128	53	-0.2
	OF	BUF	AAA	26	428	66	28	7	16	67	29	97	11	7	.282/.328/.510	107	1.6
Jake Elmore	UT	PIT	MLB	32	49	3	1	0	0	4	2	8	0	1	.213/.245/.234	87	-0.1
	UT	IND	AAA	32	414	56	31	0	6	35	37	55	3	8	.322/.387/.455	127	2.7
Erik Gonzalez	SS	IND	AAA	27	81	6	3	1	1	10	3	29	1	1	.192/.222/.295	34	-0.5
	SS	PIT	MLB	27	156	15	4	1	1	6	9	37	4	1	.254/.301/.317	66	0.1
Jack Herman	RF	GRB	A	19	300	47	12	2	13	34	28	88	6	6	.257/.340/.464	125	2.6
Corban Joseph	INF	SFN	MLB	30	17	0	0	0	0	2	1	6	0	0	.063/.118/.063	40	-0.1
	INF	PIT	MLB	30	11	1	1	0	0	0	0	1	0	0	.182/.182/.273	95	0.0
	INF	OAK	MLB	30	40	4	2	0	1	5	2	5	0	0	.189/.225/.324	87	-0.1
	INF	LVG	AAA	30	425	63	35	4	13	73	33	46	0	0	.371/.421/.585	127	1.7
Jung Ho Kang	3B	PIT	MLB	32	185	15	7	1	10	24	11	60	0	0	.169/.222/.395	75	-0.1
	3B	IND	AAA	32	31	4	3	0	1	6	4	8	0	0	.444/.516/.667	151	0.3
Pablo Reyes	LF	PIT	MLB	25	157	18	7	2	2	19	13	36	1	1	.203/.274/.322	72	-0.1
	LF	IND	AAA	25	191	22	15	0	10	30	13	37	5	3	.286/.342/.543	123	1.2
JB Shuck	OF	PIT	MLB	32	57	4	0	1	0	2	8	10	1	1	.213/.339/.255	84	0.0
	OF	IND	AAA	32	158	17	12	2	3	14	16	17	3	1	.268/.342/.444	110	1.4

Ji-Hwan Bae is a solid middle-infielder with good bat-to-ball skills and a lack of pop. He could be a player someday, but given his domestic violence conviction in Korea it might be fair to ask the Pirates if all this is really worth it. ⓘ Whatever playing time backup catcher **Steven Baron** gets will be better than the alternative, which is every pitch striking off the umpire or bouncing to the backstop. ⓘ Thrice cast off by the D'Backs, Padres and Jays before spending the majority of his season in Buffalo, **Sócrates Brito**'s chances seem to have dried up after injuries and underperformance in brief stints. "The unexamined life is not worth living," however, and Brito can only hope someone takes that to heart. ⓘ Let's not jump to conclusions and assume **Lonnie Chisenhall** really *missed* the 2019 Pirates season, but two calf strains and a broken finger left him pinin' for the fjords. He's played in 111 games over the last three seasons. ⓘ A little bit of truth in advertising for **Jake Elmore**, who made it back onto a 25-man after a two-year absence: having him in your lineup definitely helps you L more. ⓘ There's no statistic that accurately measures value added from a replacement player injuring themselves in an on-field collision, thereby resulting in missing most of the summer. Until we get to the blessed day when that changes, **Erik González** will have to settle for 50 Stanley nickels. ⓘ **Jack Herman** has become a favorite in prospect geek circles due to his low-minors performance as well as his bat speed and advanced approach. He's from Voorhees, New Jersey, but, thankfully, he was born on September 30—otherwise, we'd think he was born to be the Pumpkin King. ⚾ Yeoman infielder **Corban Joseph** had one of the more eventful transaction logs of the past year: after Oakland claimed him in the Rule 5 Draft, he made a handful of appearances for the Athletics, Giants, and Pirates during 2019. His at-bats, however, weren't nearly as interesting. ⚾ The collar-tugging decision for the Pirates to retain **Jung Ho Kang** last year looked even worse after an August release. He still has above-average exit velocity off the bat, but with a past sexual assault allegation (to say nothing of his other resolved legal issues), he probably shouldn't be playing sports right now. ⚾ Isn't it a modern baseball analysis faux pas to unironically label a player as scrappy? The algorithm is trying describe **Pablo Reyes**, an undersized utilityman with a can-do work ethic, and that's all it's spitting out. ⚾ Speedy outfield cameo artist **JB Shuck** is turning two-way. His fastball sits at 90 mph and struck out a mess of Triple-A batters in 20 innings alongside a ludicrous amount of walks.

Pitchers

PITCHER	TEAM	LVL	AGE	W	L	SV	G	GS	IP	H	HR	BB/9	K/9	K	GB%	WHIP	ERA	DRA	WARP
JT Brubaker	WEV	A-	25	0	0	0	2	2	6^2	5	0	5.4	5.4	4	42%	1.35	1.35	5.47	0.0
	IND	AAA	25	2	1	0	4	4	21	19	2	1.7	8.6	20	58%	1.10	2.57	2.85	0.8
Michael Burrows	WEV	A-	19	2	3	0	11	11	43^2	44	2	4.1	8.9	43	44%	1.47	4.33	7.40	-1.2
Blake Cederlind	BRD	A+	23	0	0	2	7	0	7^2	4	0	7.0	9.4	8	50%	1.30	1.17	3.77	0.1
	ALT	AA	23	5	1	2	31	0	45^2	31	1	3.2	8.3	42	50%	1.03	1.77	3.94	0.4
	IND	AAA	23	0	1	0	3	0	6	11	1	3.0	7.5	5	54%	2.17	7.50	8.09	-0.1
Rookie Davis	IND	AAA	26	1	6	0	13	9	52^2	61	9	3.8	6.8	40	31%	1.58	5.64	6.73	0.0
	PIT	MLB	26	0	1	0	5	1	10^2	12	3	6.8	8.4	10	48%	1.88	6.75	4.83	0.1
Montana DuRapau	IND	AAA	27	2	1	10	37	0	46^1	21	3	2.7	11.1	57	44%	0.76	2.14	1.66	2.0
	PIT	MLB	27	0	1	0	14	2	17^1	27	4	4.7	11.4	22	33%	2.08	9.35	5.38	0.0
Geoff Hartlieb	IND	AAA	25	4	1	3	26	0	39^2	31	0	3.4	11.3	50	64%	1.16	2.50	2.59	1.4
	PIT	MLB	25	0	1	0	29	0	35	52	8	4.6	9.8	38	46%	2.00	9.00	5.11	0.1
Clay Holmes	IND	AAA	26	2	1	1	10	0	15^2	17	1	8.6	7.5	13	55%	2.04	6.32	6.00	0.0
	PIT	MLB	26	1	2	0	35	0	50	45	5	6.5	10.1	56	60%	1.62	5.58	4.16	0.6
Williams Jerez	SAC	AAA	27	4	4	2	47	0	56	46	6	2.6	9.8	61	44%	1.11	3.86	2.18	2.2
	PIT	MLB	27	0	0	0	6	0	3^2	5	1	7.4	12.3	5	46%	2.18	7.36	6.83	-0.1
	SFN	MLB	27	1	0	0	6	0	6^2	7	1	8.1	5.4	4	53%	1.95	2.70	4.77	0.0
Max Kranick	BRD	A+	21	6	7	0	20	20	109^1	100	11	2.5	6.4	78	45%	1.19	3.79	4.81	0.3
James Marvel	ALT	AA	25	9	5	0	17	17	101^2	85	6	2.1	7.3	83	51%	1.07	3.10	4.51	0.5
	IND	AAA	25	7	0	0	11	11	60^2	46	4	3.3	7.9	53	49%	1.12	2.67	3.02	2.2
	PIT	MLB	25	0	3	0	4	4	17^1	25	4	3.1	4.7	9	54%	1.79	8.31	5.86	0.0
Alex McRae	IND	AAA	26	7	8	0	22	22	114^1	128	20	3.4	8.0	101	48%	1.50	5.20	5.67	1.2
	PIT	MLB	26	0	4	0	11	2	26^2	36	9	5.4	6.4	19	43%	1.95	8.77	7.12	-0.5
Dovydas Neverauskas	IND	AAA	26	3	4	9	36	0	52	51	8	3.8	12.6	73	37%	1.40	5.02	4.37	0.9
	PIT	MLB	26	0	0	0	10	0	9^1	15	2	6.8	9.6	10	35%	2.36	10.61	6.29	-0.1
Cody Ponce	ALT	AA	25	0	0	1	3	1	6	3	1	1.5	9.0	6	33%	0.67	6.00	3.11	0.1
	BLX	AA	25	1	3	1	27	0	38^1	33	1	2.8	10.3	44	57%	1.17	3.29	4.42	0.1
	IND	AAA	25	1	3	0	4	4	18^2	18	4	3.4	9.6	20	53%	1.34	5.30	3.97	0.5
Yefry Ramirez	NOR	AAA	25	1	1	0	4	4	18	11	2	4.5	12.0	24	29%	1.11	1.50	5.54	0.2
	IND	AAA	25	1	4	0	15	5	45	42	5	5.8	11.6	58	41%	1.58	5.20	4.65	0.8
	BAL	MLB	25	0	2	0	4	1	10^1	11	2	7.8	9.6	11	44%	1.94	6.97	6.15	-0.1
	PIT	MLB	25	0	0	0	9	0	14	19	2	4.5	10.3	16	56%	1.86	7.71	4.74	0.1
Yacksel Rios	LEH	AAA	26	1	3	7	31	0	34	38	4	5.8	9.8	37	50%	1.76	7.41	6.05	0.1
	IND	AAA	26	0	0	1	9	0	15^1	19	2	2.3	7.0	12	42%	1.50	2.35	6.21	0.0
	PIT	MLB	26	1	0	0	10	0	10^1	10	2	4.4	8.7	10	45%	1.45	5.23	7.55	-0.2
	PHI	MLB	26	0	0	0	4	0	2^2	6	2	10.1	6.8	2	23%	3.38	13.50	5.25	0.0
Felipe Vazquez	PIT	MLB	27	5	1	28	56	0	60	43	5	2.0	13.5	90	43%	0.93	1.65	2.32	2.0

Pittsburgh Pirates 2020

JT Brubaker missed most of 2019 with elbow woes. He's shown off enough fastball to be a potential factor in the bullpen or even the back of the rotation, and he's just about ready if healthy. ⓧ **Michael Burrows** is another overslot righty from the Northeast, with a pretty good feel and pitch mix. He'll make his full-season debut in 2020. ⓧ **Blake Cederlind** still hasn't managed to translate his triple-digit fastball into elite strikeout numbers. He did harness his control and develop his secondaries enough to move through three levels in 2019, so just a little more progress will take him to the Pittsburgh bullpen. ⓧ With only 10 2/3 innings for the Pirates last year, the most important thing about **Rookie Davis** held firm: he remained eligible for Rookie of the Year. His lack of control and penchant for getting lit up in those innings make it unlikely he gets there, but we can still dream. ⓧ He may be just organizational relief depth but **Montana DuRapau** is the first character from the *PaRappa The Rapper* series to reach the major leagues. ⓧ **Geoff Hartlieb** was the double-edged sword of feel-good stories: the former 29th-round pick made it to the Show after keeping the ball on the ground, but once there he pitched like a 29th-round pick. ⓧ **Clay Holmes** is a tall sinkerballer whose name summons images of adobe structures. Unlike mudbrick, Holmes doesn't appear to be worth building with. ⓧ The Pirates played with **Williams Jerez**'s pitch mix a little after acquiring him from the Giants late in the season, but hard-throwing lefty still looks like the quintessential taxi-squad LOOGY. ⓧ **Max Kranick** is a former overslot prep pick who was better than solid in Advanced-A with a good fastball combo and an emerging breaker, though his strikeout numbers are more Minimum Kranick. ⓧ **Travis MacGregor** has good stuff and was doing well before his elbow stopped working midway through 2018. The former second-rounder, now 22, will try and get it going again in 2020. ⓧ He's probably heard all the cinematic universe jokes in his lifetime, so we'll spare **James Marvel** and his September call-up the rod—unless he starts dating a Mrs. Maisel, then all bets are off. ⓧ **Alex McRae**'s stuff doesn't exactly play up in the bullpen, and so he'll work on winning a rotation spot in the same fashion that John Hickenlooper worked on winning the Democratic primary. ⓧ Never say never, but **Dovydas Neverauskas** is at best a sometimes pitcher: sometimes the pitch is high, sometimes it's outside. ⓧ A move to relief looked to be **Cody Ponce**'s ticket to the majors as his strikeouts spiked in his third attempt at Double-A. The Pirates had other ideas when they traded Jordan Lyles for him, putting Ponce back in the rotation and promoting him to Triple-A with mixed results. ⓧ Two pitches are enough to stick in the bullpen (fastball and changeup), just like two Y's are plenty for a first name. **Yefry Ramírez** can lay claim to both. ⓧ The Phillies waived **Yacksel Ríos** to the other side of the state last August because, despite his improved velocity, his walk rate wasn't up to the team's usual standard of yacksellence. ⓧ **Edgar Santana** might be the best reliever nobody talked about last year, but for good reason—Tommy John surgery. Expect him to return to some type of late-inning regimen, or at least the consciousness of the sport. ⓧ It's highly unlikely **Felipe Vázquez** will spend time on another professional baseball team. He was arrested and charged with the sexual assault of a 13-year-old.

Pirates Prospects

The State of the System
The NL Central is not exactly loaded with good systems. The Pirates Top Ten runs a little deeper in interesting names than their division rivals, but this out quickly after that.

The Top Ten

1 ★ ★ ★ *2020 Top 101 Prospect* **#53** ★ ★ ★
Mitch Keller   RHP   OFP: 60   ETA: 2019
Born: 04/04/96   Age: 24   Bats: R   Throws: R   Height: 6'2"   Weight: 210
Origin: Round 2, 2014 Draft (#64 overall)

The Report: We said last year in this space that Keller's fastball/curve combination was "one of the best in the minors." That remains true on raw stuff. The fastball was still sitting in the mid-90s and touching 98. The curveball still flashed plus-plus. But—and this is a pretty big "but" even for prospect writing—Keller's fastball got absolutely tattooed in the majors, like Ted Williams in his prime opposing line tattooed, and he only threw the curveball just a little over 16 percent of the time. Instead, he favored a recently-added hard slider, and while that pitch showed individual promise and was effective in a small sample, the overall package just didn't look like it was working. That slider virtually replaced Keller's change, which he'd been trying to develop for years and just wasn't getting past fringe. That leaves him with a fastball/breaking ball/breaking ball arsenal, which is a tough package to stick as a starter with, especially given sometimes wavering fastball command.

If it feels like you've heard this story before…well, the Pirates have certainly had promising young pitchers stagnate and then turn into top of the rotation arms elsewhere a few times recently. More troublingly, it seems to be immediate changes when moved to teams that are strong in pitch design, which infers that the Pirates are not maximizing incumbent talent as part of the player development process. We have no choice but to build that into Keller's report at this point, because it's already manifesting as stagnation while he's still technically prospect-eligible.

Variance: High, unusually so for a healthy player so close to graduating.

Mark Barry's Fantasy Take: Not sure if you remember, but Keller wasn't particularly good in his first taste of the big leagues. That said, he got swinging strikes a little better than league average, and even though opposing hitters treated him like a slow-pitch pitching machine, he was still a *tad* unlucky as far as his BABIP and strand rates were concerned. The ceiling might be lower, but I think there's a buying opportunity as it's likely Keller managers have quite the bitter taste lingering in their respective mouths.

────── ★ ★ ★ *2020 Top 101 Prospect* **#55** ★ ★ ★ ──────

2. Oneil Cruz SS   OFP: 60   ETA: 2021
Born: 10/04/98   Age: 21   Bats: L   Throws: R   Height: 6'7"   Weight: 175
Origin: International Free Agent, 2015

The Report: Cruz is a unicorn amongst baseball prospects, a huge young man who is far too big to play shortstop who not only plays short but still excels there. He's nimble, with good reactions and a cannon for an arm. If dropped into the majors tomorrow, he wouldn't look out of place at the position, except that he's 6-foot-7 and has substantially filled out since his listed/signing weight. Because of the unprecedented nature of his physique relative to his present defensive skills, we still have no clue where he lands defensively; he runs well enough and is agile enough that nearly anywhere in the infield or outfield is reasonably in play depending on the body development.

There's exciting upside with the stick. Cruz has monster raw power that he hasn't fully tapped into yet, but we think he's getting there. He also has unexpectedly good bat-to-ball skills given his size and aggressive MiLB assignments, which allowed him to look perfectly in place as a 20-year-old in Double-A in the second half of 2019. His levers are long and he takes a healthy cut, so there's always going to be swing-and-miss concerns present, yet they're manageable for his size and overall skill set. It's within his range of projections that he combines the feel for the bat with the raw power and turn into an offensive force.

Variance: Medium, although on the higher side of medium. It's a weird, weird group of skills and there's a lot of variance in the shape of things to come, but less in whether or not he's going to be a decent MLB regular of some form.

Mark Barry's Fantasy Take: There's not really a good comp for Cruz, because he's basically Aaron Judge minus 100 pounds, and he plays shortstop. It's not quite Judge power, but it's not-not Judge power potential. He struck out more than you'd like as he moved up the ladder, and he's still not super close, but he's an easy back-end, top-100 guy for me.

2020 Top 101 Prospect #63

3

Ke'Bryan Hayes 3B   OFP: 60   ETA: 2020
Born: 01/28/97   Age: 23   Bats: R   Throws: R   Height: 6'1"   Weight: 210
Origin: Round 1, 2015 Draft (#32 overall)

The Report: Ke'Bryan Hayes had a perfectly normal Ke'Bryan Hayes season as a 22-year-old in Triple-A and it feels...disappointing. He played to the profile and held serve as a national prospect. There's still excellent third base defense, a solid approach, good feel for contact, and plenty of doubles. Did he know they were using new baseballs? It feels like we have been waiting for the power breakout here for a while. It's easy plus raw power when he wants to show it off, he's just never consistently lifted the ball in games. I'm sure there will be other places on the list for us to grouse about Pirates prospect development, and those complaints are usually directed towards the pitching side anyway, and it seems needlessly snarky to blame them, Hayes is still a good prospect with a potential plus hit tool and plus defense. And all those laser beam doubles to left field will add up anyway.

Variance: Medium. Hayes is pretty much ready to man the hot corner in PNC Park, but how his major league game power plays out will determine if the Pirates are looking to upgrade in a few years, or if they are selling a few All-Star jerseys with "Hayes" on the back.

Mark Barry's Fantasy Take: Hayes was a dude that I long targeted as an "OMG, wait 'til he gets the to juiced balls"-type dude. Well, that didn't go particularly well. Hayes still makes a lot of contact and has a knack to get on base, but unless he adds some loft he could be a little more Brian Anderson-y as opposed to anything more interesting. That's still not bad, though.

4

Quinn Priester RHP   OFP: 60   ETA: 2023
Born: 09/15/00   Age: 19   Bats: R   Throws: R   Height: 6'3"   Weight: 195
Origin: Round 1, 2019 Draft (#18 overall)

The Report: You may have read this a few times by this point, but Priester had a case as the best prep pitcher in the 2019 draft. A cold weather arm with a good mix of projection and present stuff, Priester generally sits low-90s with his fastball at present, but with a frame that should add some good weight and a couple ticks in coming years. The pitch will flash some good sink and run, although the command can be inconsistent. The party piece here is a power 11-5, upper-70s breaking ball that consistently flashes plus. It can get a bit lazy or loopy, but we are looking at refinement here more than projection. There's the usual prep arm change, in that it exists, but it's pretty firm. You are betting on some developmental leaps once Priester gets into a professional development program, but there's also a lot to like already. You might prefer the present stuff and mid-rotation starter frame of Matt Allan. You might lean for arm strength and take Daniel Espino. Perhaps you go for what's behind door number three—the polish of Brennan Malone—but Priester is right there with all of them.

Variance: High. Leaning towards extreme given the lack of mound reps. The track record of prep righties is not great, and the command and change need grade jumps. Maybe more than one. You know the drill.

Mark Barry's Fantasy Take: You guys, it gets pretty rough pretty quickly. Priester is intriguing (especially if you play in a league that rewards Dope Names) but he's too far away and too raw to be anything more than a deep-league dart throw.

5 Cal Mitchell   RF   OFP: 55   ETA: 2021
Born: 03/08/99   Age: 21   Bats: L   Throws: L   Height: 6'0"   Weight: 209
Origin: Round 2, 2017 Draft (#50 overall)

The Report: Bradenton is an absolutely brutal place to hit, so if you were wondering that slash line above actually comes out to a bit above-average by DRC+. Yes, yes, don't scout the statline, and a bit above average isn't going to be all that special given Mitchell's limited athletic tools and corner outfield profile, but he can hit. Mitchell's swing is compact and quick, designed more for hard line drives than booming home runs, but he'll run into plenty of those as well. He can get aggressive against offspeed, but he makes enough adjustments with the barrel to project a plus hit tool, and he's strong enough to bop 20 home runs here and there along the way. He's not going to offer a ton of defensive or baserunning value, but he's perfectly fine in a corner. It's a bat-first profile that will get tested in Double-A, but so far he's handled everything pro ball has thrown at him while rarely facing a pitcher younger than him.

Variance: High. Double-A will be a stern test of the bat.

Mark Barry's Fantasy Take: To continue a long-standing tradition in these parts—can I interest you in a Jay Bruce with more strikeouts, less power and fewer walks (or say, Hunter Renfroe with way less power)?

6 Travis Swaggerty   CF   OFP: 55   ETA: 2021
Born: 08/19/97   Age: 22   Bats: L   Throws: L   Height: 5'11"   Weight: 180
Origin: Round 1, 2018 Draft (#10 overall)

The Report: If you were wondering, DRC+ likes Swaggerty's 2019 even more than Mitchell's. I have my concerns, so it's man versus machine, let's go Deep Blue. I assume Judge's torquetem sees that Swaggerty is walking more than Mitchell and striking out less, and that jibes with his amateur profile that praised his approach and bat control. I wonder if he will be too passive against better pitching, and am not a huge fan of the double toe tap timing mechanism in his swing. When Swaggerty is right, he can spray line drives from gap-to-gap and there's potential average home run power as well. And he's maintained his plus speed so far and should stick in center. It remains a rather unexciting profile that might lack a carrying tool, but a good approach, plus an average hit/power combo and a center field glove. Well you don't need Deep Blue to crunch those numbers.

Variance: Medium. In contrast to Mitchell, Swaggerty does offer some defense and baserunning value, so even if he doesn't hit a ton, there's a bench outfielder role waiting for him. By the same token, he doesn't offer Garrett-Anderson-type upside with the bat either.

Mark Barry's Fantasy Take: For fantasy, I like Swaggerty more than Mitchell and Priester. He makes contact and gets on base at a solid clip, freeing him up to use his carrying fantasy tool—those sweet, sweet wheels. More power would be nice, sure, but gimme 25-plus steals, and I'll be more than happy.

7 Cody Bolton RHP
OFP: 55   ETA: 2021
Born: 06/19/98   Age: 22   Bats: R   Throws: R   Height: 6'3"   Weight: 185
Origin: Round 6, 2017 Draft (#178 overall)

The Report: Bolton got a couple extra ticks on his fastball this year, and boy did the rest of the profile pop with the radar gun readings. The fastball sits mid-90s with some plane and he can bore it into lefties effectively. His cutterish slider in the upper-80s plays well off the fastball, and he can manipulate the offering as well, taking a little off to get a bit more depth on it. It's a potential plus two-pitch combo of power stuff. His change lags a fair bit behind at present, too firm and he struggles to turn it over. He also tired a bit late in the season despite being used fairly conservatively within his outings. So there's a chance he's a better fit in the late innings rather than taking the ball every fifth day, but the top two pitches here will play in any role.

Variance: Medium. The fastball/slider combo will get major league hitters out, but he really hasn't worked a real starter's routine/workload yet, and the change and command still need refinement.

Mark Barry's Fantasy Take: There's nothing too exciting about Bolton in a fantasy sense. Pass.

8 Tahnaj Thomas RHP
OFP: 55   ETA: 2023/24
Born: 06/16/99   Age: 21   Bats: R   Throws: R   Height: 6'4"   Weight: 190
Origin: International Free Agent, 2016

The Report: The Bahamian bats get most of the press around these parts—and to be honest I really enjoyed Trent Deveaux's recent home run derby performance—but Thomas gives the island a pretty good prospect arm to call its own. He seems like he's almost all legs. It's a high-waisted, very projectable frame that generates mid-90s heat, up to 99. The fastball barrels down on hitters from a high-three-quarters slot with good plane, and Thomas has a bit of feel for a power curve, although it's not a tight spinner yet and can get slurvy. He's athletic on the mound, but the delivery has a bit of effort and there's relief risk generally. But as projectable arm strength bets go, Thomas is one to circle at the top of your watch list.

Variance: Extreme. Thomas is a raw, Appy league arm that's mostly arm strength at present. This can go in any number of directions.

Mark Barry's Fantasy Take: Thomas is super, super raw and super, super far away, but I'd be more likely to take a chance on him putting it together than your run-of-the-mill SP5ish dude that will become a middle reliever.

9. Sammy Siani OF
OFP: 50   ETA: 2023/24
Born: 12/14/00   Age: 19   Bats: L   Throws: L   Height: 6'0"   Weight: 195
Origin: Round 1, 2019 Draft (#37 overall)

The Report: The younger brother of Michael Siani in the Reds system, Sammy shares a few familial traits on the field. He's a speedy outfielder with a loose, sweet left-handed swing that features plus bat speed and advanced barrel control. It's a hit-first profile given both his size and relative lack of loft in the swing plane, but he should make plenty of hard line drive content. He's not as advanced defensively as his older sibling, but he should be able to stick in center. There is limited physical projection here and somewhat limited upside, but outside of the lack of pop, there isn't a real weakness in Siani's game either.

Variance: High. Complex-league resume, hit-tool driven profile that hasn't seen better pitching yet. The bat really needs to be a center field profile and not a left field profile.

Mark Barry's Fantasy Take: If you want to toss Siani on your watchlist and hope he ultimately turns into Oscar Mercado with less power in a couple of years, that's perfectly respectable.

10. Lolo Sanchez OF
OFP: 50   ETA: 2022
Born: 04/23/99   Age: 21   Bats: R   Throws: R   Height: 5'11"   Weight: 168
Origin: International Free Agent, 2015

The Report: Sanchez is the sort of prospect that on a good day might look like a future table-setter at the top of a big league order, and on a bad one might look like he hasn't a prayer of escaping Double-A. His 2019 season could be split into two clean halves; one in which he tears up the Sally League and another in which he failed to find his footing down in Florida. So yes, he is like many prospects. Sanchez does have some skills in rare abundance, though. He's a natural centerfielder whose plus speed translates effortlessly into range and whose sure glove and good reads allow him to complete most plays on an easy glide. He can easily cover left and the arm should be just good enough that he can fill in at right. The speed plays well on the bases as well, and he'll steal a handful of bags. He's a very good athlete with some twitch, though he's small framed and compact without a lot of physical projection. His above-average bat speed allows him some unexpected gap power, which is augmented by his ability to take the extra base. The approach isn't terrible but he's close to a dead pull hitter who sits on pitches on the inner part of the plate, and the swing isn't the most beautiful you'll see. He has shown the ability to make adjustments in the past, however, and will flip a breaking ball the other way from time to time. Sanchez is an exciting player to watch, but his ultimate outcome will depend on how well he can continue to make those adjustments against high-level pitching.

Variance: High. Doubts abound when it comes to the hit tool, and he'll need to answer some questions even to hit his fallback role as a fourth outfielder.

Mark Barry's Fantasy Take: If you want to toss Sanchez on your watchlist and hope he ultimately turns into Oscar Mercado with less hit-tool in a couple of years, that's perfectly respectable.

The Next Ten

11 **Jared Oliva   OF**
Born: 11/27/95   Age: 24   Bats: R   Throws: R   Height: 6'3"   Weight: 203
Origin: Round 7, 2017 Draft (#208 overall)

Oliva's skillset isn't going to wow you. He was a Day 2 college pick from a major college program. He shared a lineup card at Arizona with Kevin Newman, Scott Kingery, Bobby Dalbec and J.J. Matijevic. Scouts probably weren't there to see him most weekends. This is the first time he's made one of our Pirates lists. He's had to prove it every level, and he's mostly been fine. But now he's spent a season in Double-A. He's one phone call away from the majors and you start to shift your focus to what a player can do for you major league ball club. And Oliva offers a little bit of everything.

He has a patient approach and knows how to make good contact. He picks his spots and can drive the ball the other way. There's below-average over-the-fence power, due to merely average bat speed and an emphasis on contact, but he'll hit some doubles. He can spot you in three outfield spots. He's only an average runner, but his instincts and routes play in center, and he'd be above average in a corner. You might not want him starting every day, but he can fill in for a month if someone goes down and keep the lineup moving. He's going to have to keep proving it at every level, but he's pretty close to the majors now, and surety has value too.

12 **James Marvel   RHP**
Born: 09/17/93   Age: 26   Bats: R   Throws: R   Height: 6'4"   Weight: 205
Origin: Round 36, 2015 Draft (#1087 overall)

A major-league endgame was a long time coming for Marvel. He missed his entire junior year at Duke recovering from Tommy John surgery and ended up a 36th round pick. He was always old for his level of competition, and the stuff never popped on the scouting sheet, but he kept pounding the zone with a good sinker and he beat a path to Pittsburgh while opposing hitters beat the ball into the ground. Marvel's fastball sits around 90, and shows really good late sink. It will get groundballs as long as he commands it down in the zone. He'll pop a four-seam up for a change of pace now and again too. Marvel's curve comes in either side of 80, and while he commands it well, it can lack ideal depth to get whiffs, running down barrels instead. There's also a sinking change that can run a bit too close to the sinker in both velocity and movement. Marvel's never going to rack up a ton strikeouts with his averageish stuff, but that's not really his game either. Major league hitters punished him badly when he wasn't down in the zone with everything, so he will have to tighten up his command next time around in the majors, but he should remain a backend starter candidate for Pittsburgh.

13 Jared Triolo   3B/SS
Born: 02/08/98   Age: 22   Bats: R   Throws: R   Height: 6'3"   Weight: 212
Origin: Round 2, 2019 Draft (#72 overall)

The Pirates Comp B pick out of Houston looks like he should be a power hitter, but the bat speed can be a bit on the fringy side and he tends to use his feel for the barrel to favor contact rather than try and lift the ball. He's sneaky athletic and quick for his size, so the Pirates decided to give him some reps at shortstop in the Penn League. It's an interesting experiment, and he grinds when he's there, but the skill set is a much better fit for the hot corner. He has plenty of arm for either spot and the range is above-average at third, but defensive flexibility can't hurt especially since both the hit and power tools might end up fringy.

14 Braxton Ashcraft   RHP
Born: 10/05/99   Age: 20   Bats: L   Throws: R   Height: 6'5"   Weight: 195
Origin: Round 2, 2018 Draft (#51 overall)

Ashcraft was drafted in the second round in 2018 as a projectable prep righty. The fastball hasn't popped yet, as he still mostly sits in the low-90s. The frame remains lean, and Ashcraft repeats his uptempo delivery pretty well. There's developing feel for a low-to-mid-80s slider. It's inconsistent in both shape and velocity but he will flash an above-average at the upper end of the velo band. The changeup is a work in progress but he will occasionally show one with good sink in the mid-80s. That would be decent velo separation if he could get a couple more ticks on the fastball, but we will have to wait another year for that, as the overall prospect profile remains quite raw.

15 Rodolfo Castro   2B
Born: 05/21/99   Age: 21   Bats: B   Throws: R   Height: 6'0"   Weight: 200
Origin: International Free Agent, 2015

The sort who seems to find himself posted up stubbornly on the back end of these lists year in and year out, Castro lacks a huge ceiling but is still interesting enough to warrant some words. A switch-hitter who is much more proficient from the right side, the Dominican has a loose, whippy swing that at its best sprays line drives all about the field and generates above-average gap power and decent over the fence pop. There are things that he'll have to iron out in order to improve his results from the long side of the platoon, such as his propensity to chase breaking stuff in the dirt and a tendency to pull off the ball that leaves him susceptible to hard stuff away. Well-built but sinewy with long limbs that belie his listed height of six even, Castro is more than capable at both middle-infield positions and has the arm for third if he needs it. The range is good enough and he comes in on the ball well, but his strongest trait defensively is a plus arm that plays from all sorts of angles.

16 Will Craig 1B
Born: 11/16/94   Age: 25   Bats: R   Throws: R   Height: 6'3"   Weight: 212
Origin: Round 1, 2016 Draft (#22 overall)

Craig is a tricky prospect to actually rank when you sit down to do a list. The projection here is inevitably bifurcated. He has to either hit enough to be a regular or there isn't much major league utility. There aren't gradations like there would be with, say Lolo Sanchez, a sliding scale of value. The Pirates gave Craig a handful of outfield reps in Triple-A this year, perhaps a nod to his needing positional flexibility, but he's unlikely to have the requisite speed and athleticism to play on the grass. The offensive profile remains broadly the same. There's pop, and he'll take a walk, but a stiff, long swing leads to too much swing-and-miss in the zone. Occasionally this profile hits .240, and gets on-base enough, gets enough of the power into games. But you are wishcasting for CJ Cron, and there's no room to fall short. I suppose if the Pirates really want to get creative, Craig was a solid college reliever for Wake Forest, so you might be able to carve out a Jared-Walsh-like role for him. It would certainly be more fun than watching him play right field.

17 Fabricio Macias OF
Born: 03/11/98   Age: 22   Bats: R   Throws: R   Height: 6'0"   Weight: 188
Origin: International Free Agent, 2018

Macias is essentially a less dynamic version of Lolo Sanchez, who you'll have been acquainted with earlier on in this list. He's an aggressive hitter with quick hands and a pull-heavy approach. He has the low-minors speed and power combination going, slashing and yanking hard stuff on the inner half and feasting on hanging curves. He'll steal you a base and he's managed thus far to keep his strikeouts at a reasonable clip. He's well capable of covering all three outfield positions given his good range and great arm. A sleeper prospect out of México, Macias can open some more eyes if he keeps this up against stiffer competition.

Pittsburgh Pirates 2020

18 Mason Martin   1B
Born: 06/02/99 Age: 21 Bats: L Throws: R Height: 6'0" Weight: 201
Origin: Round 17, 2017 Draft (#508 overall)

Martin may be a late-round first base only prospect but in the interest of fairness it must be noted that he is young, and he is a lefty swinger. He's performed admirably against older competition, performing well enough in the Sally to earn a mid-season promotion. The most impressive thing about Martin is his approach at the plate, which allows him to consistently work favorable counts that allow him to flex his above-average pop. The swing looks fairly rigid to me, but he nonetheless shows an ability to adjust to varying speeds, breaks, and location in order to drive the ball to all fields. He'll look weak at times against good heat up in the zone, but he's off to a promising start despite carrying an unfavorable profile.

19 Luis Escobar   RHP
Born: 05/30/96 Age: 24 Bats: R Throws: R Height: 6'1" Weight: 205
Origin: International Free Agent, 2013

The Pirates finally converted Escobar to relief in 2019 to mixed results. The fastball did pop into the mid-90s with some sink out of the pen, but the extra effort to ramp it up made him ineffectively wild at times. The bigger issue is he might not have a bat-missing secondary option. He tends to lean on his change more than his breaking ball and while it gets plenty of separation from the fastball, it only shows good fade in flashes. The curve has been even more inconsistent, although he can occasionally rips off a decent 11-5 yakker. We write a lot at the back of these team lists about 95-and-a-slider guy. Those guys can pitch in the seventh and eighth inning. Escobar needs to become a 95-and-a-something-else guy to be more than a middle reliever.

20 Matt Gorski   OF
Born: 12/22/97 Age: 22 Bats: R Throws: R Height: 6'4" Weight: 198
Origin: Round 2, 2019 Draft (#57 overall)

The Pirates second-round pick out of Indiana, Gorski has the kind of body that wouldn't look out of place in a major league outfield right now. It's close to the ideal baseball body, tall, athletic, lean and well-proportioned. He's a good runner and shouldn't fill out or slow down all that much more. There's plus raw power that can play from line-to-line. So the speed/power combo is intriguing, but the speed might not be enough to keep Gorski up the middle, and he struggles to get the power in game. There's decent bat speed, but the swing is long, and he likes to get extended. He's never really hit with wood bats and can struggle with spin. So this is more of a low-floor project than you might prefer in your college bat popped on Day One.

Personal Cheeseball

PC **Stephen Alemais SS/2B**
Born: 04/12/95   Age: 25   Bats: R   Throws: R   Height: 5'11"   Weight: 190
Origin: Round 3, 2016 Draft (#105 overall)

Alemais' season barely got started before he injured his shoulder on a slide. The injury would eventually require surgery and end his 2019 season after just 12 games. You hope there's no lingering effects for him, because boy is he fun to watch in the field. He's been a plus glove since college, and checks every box defensively—hands, actions, arm. The offensive profile is extremely Brendan Ryanish, and while the glove is good, it isn't THAT good. Alemais might even have less power than Ryan too. Don't ever bet against a good shortstop making the majors, but I also won't be complaining too much if I get a look at Alemais' slick glovework around the Eastern or International League circuit in 2020.

Low Minors Sleeper

LMS **Colin Selby RHP**
Born: 10/24/97   Age: 22   Bats: R   Throws: R   Height: 6'1"   Weight: 218
Origin: Round 16, 2018 Draft (#474 overall)

A 16th-rounder last year out of D-III Randolph-Macon, Selby put up good numbers backed up by good stuff and at 21 was age-appropriate for the Sally League. Listed at 6-foot-1, the righty is sturdily built without much projection remaining. This is fine, as he already holds his velo at 94 mph late into outings and can hit as high as 97 early. He also has a nascent four-pitch mix, with secondary offerings of varying efficacy. He looks to have both a slider and a curve, in the mid and low 80s, respectively, but they do blend at times. The former doesn't have a whole lot of bite, though he can drop it in for strikes especially to the gloveside against right-handed hitters. The latter is effective as a chase pitch in the dirt, at least at this level. He also throws a change that often comes in firm around 90 but occasionally shows split action. Long way to go but could end up a steal considering where they got him, even if he ends up a middle reliever.

Top Talents 25 and Under (as of 4/1/2020)

1. Mitch Keller
2. Oneil Cruz
3. Ke'Bryan Hayes
4. Bryan Reynolds
5. Cole Tucker
6. Quinn Priester
7. Travis Swaggerty
8. Cody Bolton
9. Tahnaj Thomas
10. Sammy Siani

There's all of two players on this list who have exhausted their prospect eligibility. A year ago, Reynolds checked in at No. 9 in the Pirates' system, while Tucker was No. 6. In their respective rookie seasons, Reynolds put up a 110 DRC+ that shows his .317 batting average wasn't entirely fluky despite an obscene .387 BABIP. He's hit at every level, including now the majors, and while his ceiling is probably what we saw in 2019, that's an above-average corner outfielder by any stretch of the imagination.

Tucker didn't see as much playing time as Reynolds and scuffled in a 159-plate appearance cup of coffee, but we're still talking about someone who is likely to stick at shortstop as something resembling a second-division starter.

Neither Reynolds nor Tucker have quite the upside of the trio that dots the top of the list, but as the Pirates enter what's looking like a painful couple of years, they're likely to both be quality major leaguers the other youngsters will meet in Pittsburgh in the coming years.

Part 3: Featured Articles

The Baseball Is Juiced (Again)

Robert Arthur

This article originally appeared at Baseball Prospectus on April 5, 2019.

It started when the normally reliable Chris Sale got lit up for three homers by the Mariners in the Red Sox's season opener. It was part of a record number of taters that flew on Opening Day, as starters from Sale to Zack Greinke were taken deep by the handful. Then Christian Yelich hit a home run in each of his first four games, tying yet another MLB record, this one for consecutive games with a dinger to start a season.

It didn't take long for fans and players to begin whispering and tweeting about the baseballs being juiced again. It's early yet for us to come to any definitive conclusion about the 2019 season, but preliminary data shows that the baseball has returned to its aerodynamic peak. Whether that means this season will smash home run records like 2017 did remains to be seen.

Before home run explosion over the last few years, no one worried too much about the baseball's air resistance. While MLB and Rawlings (the company that manufactures the official baseballs) kept track of dozens of metrics to make sure that the ball was consistent from month to month, they didn't measure drag.

But drag is incredibly important in determining how likely a hitter is to knock one out of the park. As baseballs become more aerodynamic, they travel further given a certain initial velocity. A deep fly ball that might have been caught at the warning track can instead go into the first row of the stands. A three percent change in drag coefficient can work to add about five feet to a well-hit fly ball, which can in turn increase home runs league wide by an astounding 10-15 percent.

It's possible to measure the aerodynamics of the baseball using the pitch-tracking radars currently in place in each MLB ballpark. By calculating the loss of speed from when the pitch is released to when it crosses the plate, you can directly measure the drag coefficient on the baseball. I first wrote about the role of decreasing drag in boosting home runs in 2017, and MLB's commission of scientists and statisticians later confirmed that the more aerodynamic baseballs

Pittsburgh Pirates 2020

in use that year were largely to blame for the spike in home runs. The same commission rejected some alternate hypotheses, like rising temperatures and a league-wide boost in launch angle pushing more balls over the fence.

The current era has featured some large fluctuations in drag coefficient, leading to first an explosion in 2016 and 2017, and then a dialing back of homers last year. Curious about the record-breaking home run tallies in the last few days, I used the same methodology to measure the aerodynamics of the baseballs so far in 2019.

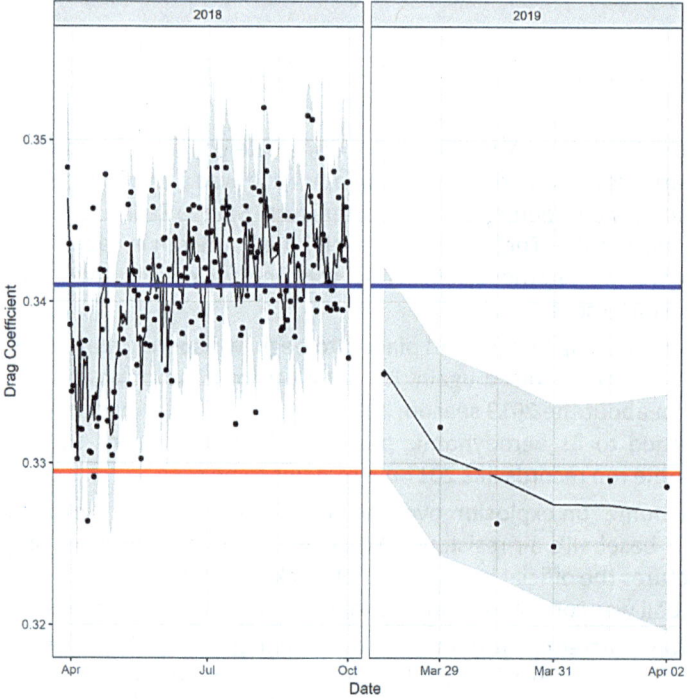

We're only a week into the 2019 season, but the drag numbers so far are among the lowest recorded in the last calendar year. With apologies for gory math, the current 2019 season average drag coefficient (the red line) would be below the 95 percent credible interval (the shaded area) for about nine-tenths of the 2018 season. (I used a Bayesian Random Walk model implemented in INLA to calculate these credible intervals, averaging the drag numbers in each game and adjusting for park.)

There were only a handful of six-day stretches in 2018 that had drag numbers below what we're seeing now, and most were in late June and early July. All of this means that 2019's data so far is quite a bit different than what we saw through most of last year.

128 - The Baseball Is Juiced (Again)

These drag coefficients factor out the effects of temperature and air density, so they aren't a product of April cold. However, the numbers could be deceptive if the radars used to track pitches have changed from year to year. I consulted with some experts within baseball who were not aware of any specific modifications to the radar this year that could produce this pattern, but it's an important caveat of which to be aware.

On the one hand, it's only been six days, and we don't quite have the statistical basis to say that these drag coefficients are unprecedented compared to 2018. On the other hand, we've witnessed about 5,000 fastballs so far this season, so it's not as if our sample size is small. At least so far, the baseball has played like it's much more aerodynamic than it was last year. In fact, the current drag coefficient is really only comparable to 2017, when the baseballs were more aerodynamic than they had been in at least a decade.

It's not just fancy radar tracking indicating that the baseball is flying through the air more easily. The current number of home runs per game (as of this writing) is the highest it's been since the heady days of 2017, the year that teams and players broke dinger-related records everywhere you looked. That's especially remarkable considering that we're in what is typically the coldest part of the regular season, when lower temperatures and higher winds tend to suppress offense and keep balls in the air within the park. Comparing only from April to April, this year's rate of home runs per fly ball is even a little bit higher than it was in 2017.

With that said, the current measurements are no guarantee that 2019 will be another year of record-shattering homer hitting. The trouble with the drag measurements is that they are not consistent from June to August, from week to week, or even sometimes from day to day. Whether because of natural manufacturing variation or differences in the underlying supplies of cowhide and thread that go into the baseballs, drag has a tendency to fluctuate up and down over the course of a year. So the homers that fly in the first week of April wouldn't necessarily clear the fence a week later.

It's possible that this one-week drop in drag coefficient subsides and the baseball returns to its 2018 levels. On the other hand, it's almost equally probable that the ball becomes even more slippery and flies ever farther. Either way, it's clear that the baseball's air resistance is something to keep an eye on for the remainder of the 2019 season.

—*Robert Arthur is an author of Baseball Prospectus.*

The Moral Hazard of Playing It Safe

Craig Goldstein

This article originally appeared at Baseball Prospectus on August 6, 2019.

A couple days prior to the trade deadline, amidst a sea of tranquility posing as the lead up to the trade deadline, Bob Nightengale took to Twitter. Nightengale, who was probably wearing his pants backwards at the time, tweeted that MLB GMs were coming around on the idea that the unified trade deadline should be moved back from July 31 to August 15, so they could better assess their positions in the standings and whether they should buy or sell. To which I said:

This might strike some as reductive and churlish. And it might be that, but it isn't really wrong, either. Jeff Quinton wrote a great piece discussing the environmental factors that enable front offices to avoid risk without upsetting the apple cart within their own fanbases. I don't believe that it goes far enough, however. His article gives us the proper framework through which to understand why these behaviors have been allowed to seep into front offices throughout the league. Understanding the reasons behind these actions are different from excusing them, though, and GMs should not be let off the hook for their non-competitive approach to the trade deadline (much less the offseason).

⚾ ⚾ ⚾

It's fair to say that fans as a group have rarely, if ever, been pro-player. It is also fair to say that in the time during and following the Moneyball revolution, the pendulum swung from fans who cared intensely about winning in the moment (and thus might be intolerant of a rebuilding approach) to fans who supported building a team that could compete throughout multiple seasons, viewing the playoffs as a crapshoot, with the thought that getting multiple bites at the apple was a better approach than taking a bigger bite in any one season.

There's nothing wrong with that approach, and I still find merit in that argument. However, it seems that the pendulum has swung too far in that direction. Teams are overvaluing some of the individual factors that make themselves long-term contenders rather than attempting to seize a championship when given the opportunity. It's a difficult needle to thread.

And surely, they (and those in similar positions) would have liked another two weeks to clarify where they stand so as to better marshal their resources. We've all asked for a few more minutes when staring at a menu. But all of these GMs and front office personnel are where they are to make difficult decisions. They have proprietary data and internal analysts dedicated to understanding their position relative to the rest of the league, and how any move in the here and now impacts their long-term vision. To complain (if that report is accurate) that over half the season is not enough to properly assess their season is bullshit of the highest order. Move the deadline, and you'd simply have increasingly discounted trade offers because teams would be acquiring even less control of anyone they're acquiring, rental or not.

Major league front offices are behaving like the managers they lampooned two decades ago. They're effectively sacrificing a runner to second in the ninth inning—not because it's the correct move, but rather because it is safe. It used to be that the phrase "moral hazard" was used to describe general managers who made ill-fated, short-sighted decisions aimed at locking in wins and securing their jobs at the expense of their team's future. Now, general managers are guilty of committing moral hazards in the opposite direction, playing it utterly safe and terrified of becoming scapegoats.

In lieu of bold action, they opt to pussyfoot around a current window of contention, choosing instead to play the long game and stack up years of control like they're blocks in a game of Jenga. GMs pass on signing quality players in free agency because the back-end of the deal might look bad, and because they might be able to squeeze out 70 percent of the production from a player who costs a tenth as much. That's a safer investment, too, because it's also hard to prove a negative—it's impossible to prove that Manny Machado would make the Mets a playoff team in 2019-2020, but it's easy to say that the back half of Robinson Cano's contract sucks. Owners, who rule over GM's jobs, are also humans with human brain processes that will always make the so-called albatross contract uglier than the road not taken.

These days, GMs are remembered for the bad deals they make and the surplus value they generate, not the acquisition of expensive, necessary talents that meet their market worth (or fall slightly short while still providing significant on-field value). And front offices know that one or two expensive misfires can cost them their jobs, no matter how many good deals they make.

No front office exemplifies this ethos more than the Toronto Blue Jays. General Manager Ross Atkins had this to say following the Blue Jays underwhelming trade deadline:

This is by no means the first time that an executive will cite years of control to justify their actions, which is often just another way of saying "don't look at what we got, look at how much we got of it." Atkins touts quantity to elide the discussion of quality—either, that of the players acquired, or those given up. Remember: the other teams presumably value years of control, too.

Atkins also had some thoughts to offer regarding free agents back in early 2018:

This ignores, of course, whether the player can create enough value in the front end of a contract to justify the longer term of a deal, and the decline that often occurs in the back end. It also ignores whether the player can fill a need the team requires and put them in a position to compete for and win a championship. But as teams seemingly avoid contention at all, where they might end up having to consider and later justify some of these tough decisions, we still see risk-averse approaches.

Anthony Fenech's article on two trades that recently extended GM Al Avila didn't make got at this issue rather well:

> Passing on those deals was defensible: Both players had yet to break out and trading [Michael] Fulmer—a pitcher who appeared to be a future ace, no matter his injury concerns—would have taken serious gumption, opening Avila up to strong criticism.

Avoiding strong criticism is something each of us can understand as a motivation, but the avoidance of criticism only matters if that criticism is valid. In Fulmer's case, shoving his injury concerns aside affects not only the years that the team controls him (he is currently missing a full season due to Tommy John surgery) but also the quality of those seasons, as his knee and elbow injuries combined to dampen his effectiveness even when healthy enough to pitch. But it was easy to present the then-current image of Fulmer as a top of the rotation pitcher who the team had under its domain for the next five seasons as something to build around. The status quo isn't nearly as often second-guessed as a decision that disrupts it.

⚾ ⚾ ⚾

MLB GMs are risk-averse to a fault. They are ivy-educated and consulting firm-approved, and yet they can't seem to avoid leaving wins on the table in their all-consuming lust for a non-existent $/WAR championship. They are supposed to zig when everyone else zags, and not merely pay lip service to the idea of zigging through a calculated PR plan built on convincing the fan base their approach is novel when it actually apes most of their competitors. Instead they've become far more concerned with making safe, accepted-by-the-new-common-wisdom decisions, such that our prior understanding of what a moral hazard is has become inverted.

I can't blame them entirely, and not only because of the reasons that Quinton illuminated in his article, but also because of the damage wrought by the introduction of the second wild card (WC2) spot. MLB's desire to have more teams in playoff contention has sparked anti-competitive behavior. Teams know now that they do not need to swing big as they assemble their roster because there is a good chance that a mediocre team can either catch fire and capture a division, or muddle along until they back into the WC2.

Simultaneously, the one-game playoff has neutered the WC1, putting an entire season on the flip of a coin like some sort of baseball-obsessed Anton Chigurh. While the one-game playoff makes sense as a way to increase the value of winning a division, it also means that if a front office doesn't like its chances of overcoming a behemoth like the Dodgers or Astros in the offseason, they have few incentives to chase glory. Similarly, the relative inaction in the NL Central at the trade deadline—despite a wide open division—can be explained by the idea that any high-variance investment could still result in only a wild card (or worse) result, given the mere two months left in the season to make an impact.

⚾   ⚾   ⚾

As stated at the top, we should not confuse reasons for excuses. The implementation of the second wild card is just one of many environmental factors that influence how each front office operates. I am convinced that it is one of the larger factors, but I am also convinced that organizations need to shed the yoke of "efficiency at all costs" so that they can instead pursue competition, as the spirit of the game intends. Until they do, we're all deadline losers.

—*Craig Goldstein is an author of Baseball Prospectus.*

Index of Names

Alemais, Stephen 123	Hartlieb, Geoff 109
Archer, Chris 46	Hayes, Ke'Bryan 89, 115
Ashcraft, Braxton 99, 120	Heredia, Guillermo 26
Bae, Ji-Hwan 107	Herman, Jack 107
Baron, Steven 107	Holland, Derek 62
Bell, Josh 18	Holmes, Clay 109
Bido, Osvaldo 100	Howard, Sam 64
Bolton, Cody 101, 117	Jennings, Steven 103
Brault, Steven 48	Jerez, Williams 109
Brito, Socrates 107	Joseph, Corban 107
Brubaker, JT 109	Kang, Jung Ho 107
Burdi, Nick 50	Kela, Keone 66
Burrows, Michael 109	Keller, Mitch 68, 113
Cabrera, Melky 20	Kramer, Kevin 90
Castro, Rodolfo 85, 120	Kranick, Max 109
Cederlind, Blake 109	Kuhl, Chad 104
Craig, Will 86, 121	Macias, Fabricio 121
Crick, Kyle 52	Maile, Luke 28
Cruz, Oneil 87, 114	Martin, Jason 91
Davis, Rookie 109	Martin, Mason 92, 122
Del Pozo, Miguel 54	Marvel, James 109, 119
DuRapau, Montana 109	McRae, Alex 109
Dyson, Jarrod 22	Mitchell, Cal 93, 116
Elmore, Jake 107	Moran, Colin 30
Erlin, Robbie 56	Musgrove, Joe 70
Escobar, Luis 58, 122	Neverauskas, Dovydas 109
Feliz, Michael 60	Newman, Kevin 32
Florez, Santiago 102	Noesi, Héctor 72
Frazier, Adam 24	Oliva, Jared 94, 119
Gonzalez, Erik 107	Osuna, José 34
Gorski, Matt 88, 122	Peguero, Liover 95

Pittsburgh Pirates 2020

Polanco, Gregory 36	Stallings, Jacob 40
Ponce, Cody 109	Stratton, Chris 76
Priester, Quinn 105, 115	Swaggerty, Travis 98, 116
Ramirez, Yefry 109	Taillon, Jameson 78
Reyes, Pablo 107	Thomas, Tahnaj 106, 117
Reynolds, Bryan 38	Tilson, Charlie 42
Rios, Yacksel 109	Triolo, Jared 120
Rodríguez, Richard 74	Tucker, Cole 44
Sanchez, Lolo 96, 118	Vazquez, Felipe 109
Selby, Colin 123	Wang, Wei-Chung 80
Shuck, JB 107	Williams, Trevor 83
Siani, Sammy 97, 118	